P9-ARQ-282

DISCARD

HIRAM HALLE MEMORIAL LIBRARY
271 Westchester Avenue
Pound Ridge, New York
10576-1714

GERMANY

DISCARD

GERMANY

DISCARD

Sean Dolan

CHELSEA HOUSE PUBLISHERS
Philadelphia

FRONTISPIECE: The 1897 Rathaus (city hall) in Hamburg.

Chelsea House Publishers
Contributing Author: Derek Davis

Copyright © 1999 by Chelsea House Publishers,
a division of Main Line Book Co.
All rights reserved.
Printed and bound in the United States of America.

First Printing

1   3   5   7   9   8   6   4   2

Library of Congress Cataloging-in-Publication Data

Dolan, Sean.
Germany / Sean Dolan.
p.   cm. — (Major world nations)
Includes index.
Summary: An introduction to the geography, history, government, economy, people, and culture of Germany.
ISBN 0-7910-4752-0
1. Germany—Juvenile literature.   [1. Germany.]
I. Title.   II. Series.
DD258.3.D65   1990
943—dc20   90-2307
CIP
AC

CONTENTS

FACTS AT A GLANCE

Land and People

Official Name Federal Republic of Germany

Capital Berlin (population 3.5 million)

Seat of Government Bonn (population 300,000)

Other Major Cities Hamburg (population 1.7 million); Munich (population 1.3 million); Cologne (population 950,000); Frankfurt (population 660,000); Essen (population 620,000); Dorfmund (population 600,000); Stuttgart (population 600,000)

Language German

Area 137,826 square miles (356,970 square kilometers)

Population 84 million

Population Density 606 per square mile (234 per square kilometer)

Religion Roughly 45 percent Catholic, 37 percent Protestant, 18 percent unaffiliated or other

Highest Point The Zugspitze, 9,721 feet (2,963 meters)

Mountain Ranges Bavarian Alps, Swabian Jura, Weser Mountains, Harz Mountains, Thüringer Wald

Major Rivers Danube, Rhine, Main, Elbe, Weser, Oder

Economy

Currency	Mark, divided into 100 pfennigs
Chief Agricultural Products	Wheat, barley, potatoes, beets, pork, beer, wine
Major Industries	Manufacturing (vehicles, electrical equipment, iron and steel products, chemicals, heavy machinery, construction), commerce, banking
Natural Resources	Iron, hard coal, lignite, potash, natural gas

Government

Form	Constitutional democracy
Suffrage	All citizens 18 years and older
Legislative Assembly	Two chambers: Bundestag (lower house, elected by popular vote); Bundesrat (upper house, appointed by governments of the Länder, or states)
Head of Government	Chancellor, head of the party or coalition maintaining a working majority in the Bundestag
Head of State	President, chosen by popular election
Political Divisions	16 Länder (states)

HISTORY AT A GLANCE

1st century	Germanic tribesmen commanded by Arminius maul Roman legions at the Battle of Teutoburger Wald.
410	Rome is sacked by Visigoths led by Alaric.
732	Charles Martel defeats the Moors at the Battle of Tours.
800	Charlemagne is crowned emperor by Pope Leo III.
936–73	Otto I reigns as king of Germany; he founds Holy Roman Empire and expands the geographic extent of Germany.
1076	Pope Gregory VII excommunicates Heinrich IV.
1122	Heinrich V cedes power of investiture at Concordat of Worms.
1152–90	Friedrich I (Barbarossa) reigns as Holy Roman Emperor.
1215–50	Friedrich II rules the Holy Roman Empire; he grants increased power to Germany's bishops and nobility and adds much new territory to Germany.

1356	Golden Bull formalizes the procedure for electing the Holy Roman Emperor.
ca. 1400	Extensive eastward migration of German-speaking people begins.
1438	Albert II is crowned Holy Roman Emperor; he is the first Habsburg emperor of the dynasty that will rule until 1806.
1455	Johannes Gutenberg develops the first printing press.
1528	The death of Albrecht Dürer, the great German painter, printmaker, and theoretician.
1618–48	The Thirty Years' War rages in Germany.
1701	Friedrich I is crowned king of Prussia.
1740–63	Friedrich II, or Frederick the Great, leads Prussia to victory in the War of the Austrian Succession and the Seven Years' War.
1774	Johann Wolfgang von Goethe's *The Sorrows of Young Werther* is published.
1806	Napoléon Bonaparte invades Germany and abolishes the Holy Roman Empire.
1815	Diplomats at the Congress of Vienna establish the Confederation of Germany, thereby ensuring continued German political fragmentation.
1827	Composer Ludwig van Beethoven dies.
1862	Kaiser Wilhelm I appoints Otto von Bismarck chancellor of Prussia.
1866	Prussia defeats Austria in the Austro-Prussian War.
1870–71	Bismarck goads France into war; Prussia's victory leads to formation of a unified German state under Prussian leadership.
1890	Kaiser Wilhelm II dismisses Bismarck; Bismarck dies in 1898.

1914–18	World War I is fought; Germany is defeated.
1919–33	The Weimar Republic governs during a period of ruinous economic troubles. The Expressionism movement reaches its peak.
1933	Adolf Hitler becomes chancellor of Germany and quickly assumes dictatorial powers.
1933–45	Hitler imprisons and kills millions of European Jews; Germany is defeated in World War II.
1949	Germany is divided into two states: The Federal Republic of Germany (West Germany), under the control of the United States, England, and France, embraces democracy and capitalism. The German Democratic Republic (East Germany), under the control of the Soviet Union, adopts state-controlled communism.
1961	East German government builds the Berlin Wall to slow emigration to West Germany.
1971–73	West German chancellor Willy Brandt and East German leader Erich Honecker agree to mutual recognition of their countries.
1985	Mikhail Gorbachev, new Soviet leader, loosens Soviet control over Eastern Europe and encourages reforms.
1989–90	Grassroots pressure for reform escalates into the sudden collapse of the East German government. The Berlin Wall falls, and East Germany unites with West Germany under the West German constitution.
1994	After an economic slump, the united Germany begins to recover from the absorption of the East German economy.

Chancellor Helmut Kohl applauds during a debate in the German parliament. Kohl led the reunited Germany through its rapid progress in the 1990s.

1

Germany and the World

The history of Germany in the 20th century has been a roller coaster of alternating pride and humiliation, aggression and defeat, despair and regeneration. Along the way, the country helped provoke two world wars that brought a human and material devastation unparalleled in history. Yet, today, Germany stands as something of a model of both economic and social progress, a reminder that a nation's people can lift themselves from the depths of misery to attain both hope for the future and some understanding of the errors of the past.

During World War II (1939–45), Germany under Adolf Hitler and his National Socialist German Workers party—the *Nazis*—unleashed a horrific reign of terror across Europe. Eventually Germany, along with its partners Italy and Japan, was defeated by the Grand Alliance, a coalition of nations including the United States, Great Britain, France, and the Soviet Union. Then, after the war, on the basis of decisions made during the war by the victorious Allied leaders, both Germany and its capital city, Berlin, were divided into four sectors, each administered by one of the Allied powers.

By this time, unfortunately, the cooperation between the Soviet Union and the Western Allies was breaking down into mutual suspicion, and the 45-year-long *cold war* was beginning. In the simplest terms, the cold war pitted the concepts of democracy and a capitalist, free-market economy (promoted by the United States in particular) against the Communist notion of a state-administered economy (represented by the Soviet Union). The stakes were the political and ideological dominance of Europe—and, by extension, the world.

The divided, defeated Germany was caught up in the emerging cold war. The Soviet-dominated sector of Germany soon diverged sharply from the sectors controlled by the Western Allies, and in 1949, in response to the realities of the American-Soviet struggle, Germany was formally separated into two nations. This sundering symbolized all too starkly the larger division of Europe itself into opposing camps of East and West.

The German Democratic Republic (East Germany), created from the Soviet sector, remained under close Soviet control for the 41 years of its existence. The other three powers merged their sectors into the Federal Republic of Germany (West Germany), retaining nominal oversight at first but allowing West Germans practical control over both their government and their destiny.

West Germany adopted the ideals of freedom of association and speech (with some limits), private ownership, and an open economy. Soon West Germany blossomed economically and politically, producing the *Wirtschaftwunder*—the "economic miracle"—that would turn it into one of the world's three great economies, along with the United States and Japan. By contrast, East Germany was centrally controlled in its politics and economic policies, and strict limits were placed on basic freedoms such as speech, association, and movement. However, East Germany provided its citizens with all basic necessities—shelter, jobs, health care, and comprehensive education—through state-run industries and institutions, and it maintained the most productive economy in Soviet-dominated Eastern Europe.

The most demoralizing symbol of the East-West division was the Berlin Wall, constructed by the East German government in 1961 to stem the continuing flow of refugees to the West. This barrier, 103 miles (165 kilometers) long, stood for over a quarter-century as a monument to the political failure to compromise.

At long last, Mikhail Gorbachev, who became the Soviet leader in 1985, began to loosen Soviet control over the Eastern European "satellite" countries, including East Germany. In response, long-suppressed workers and political dissidents in Eastern Europe flexed their muscles. Soon there were signs of unrest, followed by demands for total freedom from the Soviets. The entrenched, monolithic government of East Germany, alone among the major Communist nations, resisted Gorbachev's call for reform, causing increasing resentment among its citizens.

During the late 1980s, Gorbachev began the withdrawal of Soviet troops and influence from Eastern Europe. In one of the more amazing debacles in history, this voluntary retreat snowballed into a total Soviet collapse, ending in the abolition of the Soviet Union itself in 1991 and its division into a group of independent nations. By that time, East Germany had undergone an equally rapid dissolution. In 1989, limited protests by hundreds of young East German dissidents had swelled within weeks to massive rallies of up to half a million strong, demanding reforms and an easing of the almost total ban on travel to the West. When the East German government, in an attempt at conciliation, relaxed travel restrictions, tens of thousands of East Germans swarmed across the border. On November 9, 1989, Berliners took sledgehammers to the hated Berlin Wall and began reducing it to rubble.

Bowing to this pressure, East Germany announced free elections for March 1990, and the elections were won by a conservative coalition that favored reunification with West Germany. On October 3, 1990, Germany became once again a single country—united under the West German constitution, known as the Basic Law.

Ever since the bitter division of the country in 1949, "reunification" of the two Germanys had been a Western rallying cry. After more than three decades, however, both East and West Germany had developed economies deeply wedded to their differing world views. Also, despite the peaceful behavior of both Germanys since World War II, victims of German brutality in the two world wars—which included virtually every nation of Europe—feared that a strong Germany might revert to its "natural" aggressive streak.

Yet the reality of reunification has been both remarkable and heartening. The unified German economy enjoyed an immediate boom, fueled by Easterners' demand for consumer goods, before falling into an unavoidable slump as the German government worked to shore up the weaker Eastern economy and rebuild the

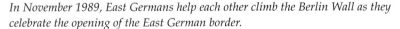

In November 1989, East Germans help each other climb the Berlin Wall as they celebrate the opening of the East German border.

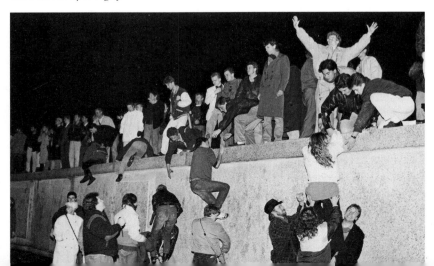

Johann Wolfgang von Goethe (1749–1832), poet, dramatist, novelist, and philosopher, is often considered the most important German writer. Goethe was a compassionate and vulnerable individual who grappled with a wide variety of human problems.

decaying infrastructure. More troubling during this period were neo-Nazi attacks against immigrants and foreign workers. Since the mid-1990s, however, both problem areas have come under greater control. Today, Germany appears on the road to lasting political and economic stability.

A "Problematical Endowment"

Germany has long been a mystery and a torment, both to its neighbors and to itself. Wrote Thomas Mann, generally considered the greatest of German novelists, "Whosoever should strive to transform Germany . . . would be trying to rob her of her best and weightiest quality, of her problematical endowment, which is the essence of her nationality."

The "problematical" nature of Germany's national identity has been a dominant theme in German literature, art, and music for centuries. For example, Johann von Goethe, whose poems, plays, and fiction made him the most significant figure of the Romantic period (1790–1850), noted that "the Germans make everything difficult, both for themselves and for everyone else."

Without question, Germany has a great cultural heritage. Authors such as Mann, Goethe, Johann Christoph Schiller (a contemporary of Goethe), and 20th-century playwright Bertolt Brecht represent but one aspect of Germany's proud legacy. In addition to its rich, varied literature, Germany produced the music of Johann Sebastian Bach, who revolutionized music in the Baroque period; of Ludwig van Beethoven, perhaps the most famous name in classical music; and of many later 19th-century composers, including Robert Schumann, Richard Wagner, and Johannes Brahms. (Wagner, especially in his operas, expressed an almost obsessive longing for German identity that foreshadowed the nationalistic excesses of the 20th century.)

Similarly, the paintings of Albrecht Dürer, Lucas Cranach the Elder, Hans Holbein the Younger, and Matthias Grünewald remain among the highest embodiments of medieval and Renaissance art. The philosophical treatises of Gottfried Leibniz, Immanuel Kant, Johann Fichte, and Georg Wilhelm Hegel changed the course of Western thought.

What then, in Mann's view, is unsettling or "problematical" about the German people? And why did Goethe believe that the Germans make things "difficult" for themselves and others? German history helps provide the answers. One characteristic that history reveals is the fierce German military spirit. The earliest recorded view of that spirit dates from the Roman Empire of 2,000 years ago, which was unable to subdue the Germanic tribes during its centuries of expansion. Later, in the 5th century, such warlike German bands as the Vandals pushed the tottering Roman Empire to ruin, sacking Rome itself.

During the 17th century, the Thirty Years' War, fought on German soil (though often among non-German combatants), produced ruination unsurpassed until the Nazi regime of World War II. In the following century, the forces of the German state of Prussia, commanded by the enlightened despot Friedrich II—"Frederick the Great"—twice overran central and eastern Europe. During the War of the Austrian Succession (1740–48) and the Seven Years' War (1756–63), his troops occupied much of present-day Hungary, Poland, Romania, and the Czech Republic. In both cases, German aggression sparked the wars, and bloodshed and destruction accompanied the Prussian troops on their conquests.

Though a cultured person who wrote music and poetry and implemented progressive social legislation in his kingdom, Friedrich II was a cunning military strategist, ruthless in battle. "Dogs! Would you live forever?" he was said to shout at Prussian infantrymen slow to throw themselves into combat.

Barely 100 years after the close of the Seven Years' War, Prussia turned its sights westward and invaded the neighboring nation of France. Victory was swift—the French capital of Paris fell in 1871, about five months after the war began—and resulted in the formation of the German Empire, the first truly unified German political entity. France was forced to hand over the provinces of Alsace and Lorraine, which were not returned until the Treaty of Versailles following World War I.

But Germany unleashed its greatest aggressions in the 20th century. When the German kaiser (emperor), Wilhelm II, backed Austria-Hungary in its declaration of war against the Balkan nation of Serbia in 1914, a conflagration began that devastated most of Europe. German forces soon invaded France, Belgium, and Russia, and casualties on both sides reached catastrophic proportions. By the end of World War I, in November 1918, an estimated 10 million Europeans and Americans had been killed. More than twice that number had been wounded, and the economic and spiritual damage to the European continent was impossible to estimate.

At war's end, the European nations met, as they had several times in the past, to consider how to rein in or neutralize Germany. The resulting Treaty of Versailles (1919) placed all blame for the war on Germany and demanded reparations so huge that they undermined the entire German economy. Preying on racial fears, economic disturbances, and German resentment at being made the scapegoat for World War I, Adolf Hitler rose to power in part by fanning the ever-warlike German spirit. Named chancellor in 1933, Hitler and his Nazi party quickly assumed dictatorial powers, crushed all opposition, and embarked on yet another program of German conquest.

In 1938 Hitler annexed Austria and bullied the European powers into giving him a portion of Czechoslovakia. His invasion of Poland in September of the following year began World War II, just 21 years after the end of World War I, which had supposedly been the "war to end all wars." Hitler's plan to establish a Third German *Reich* (empire) included his so-called "final solution": the extermination of all European Jews, whom he blamed for Germany's economic woes and for supposedly infecting the pure German stock with their racial inferiority. After six years, the combined military might of the United States, Great Britain, France, and the Soviet Union subdued Hitler's Germany. By that time, much of Europe had again been reduced to rubble. Six million Jews, as well the mentally and physically disabled and most European Gypsies, had been put to death in Hitler's concentration camps through his program of extermination known as the *Holocaust.*

This brief sketch of German history makes it clear why Mann and Goethe, and others like them, have used terms like "problematical" and "difficult" to describe Germany. Although not denying the majesty of Germany's cultural achievement, many writers, historians, and psychologists have suggested that Germany's military excesses derive not just from historical and economic forces but from fundamental aspects of the German character. They theorize that the German love of order, respect for authority, and social conformity have made Germans particularly susceptible to authoritarian government and unlikely to protest when that government exceeds the bounds of constitutional behavior and human decency. Some hold that Germans tend to worship power, especially military might, for its own sake.

In the years following the *Stunde Null*, or zero hour, in 1945, when the German people awoke to discover their government toppled, their cities bombed into mounds of debris, and their land occupied by four foreign victors, the question of national identity took on increased significance. West Germany's recovery from the ravages of World War II was an astounding example of determination and dedication, testimony to the many positive features of German character. Still, the past continued to haunt the German national consciousness, and the division of Germany into East and West only intensified the problem.

Today, the reunited Germany—following the temporary chaos of its reunion—appears set to remain in the forefront of the world's most progressive and prosperous nations. In the social arena, many Germans have moved beyond postwar attempts to suppress knowledge of Hitler's crimes and deny their collective guilt. Now they are making a more conscious effort to come to terms with their country's past episodes of violence—and to move beyond them.

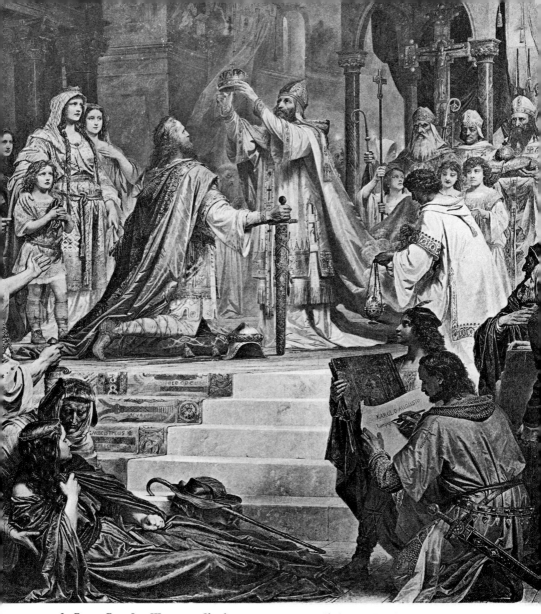

In Rome, Pope Leo III crowns Charlemagne emperor on Christmas Day in 800. As emperor, Charlemagne—who was a champion of Christianity—assumed jurisdiction over the Roman Empire, set up an efficient administrative system by which to rule his empire, and had the law of his domain codified.

2

Like None but Themselves

Literary observation of the unique character of the Germans began early. Writing in the first century A.D., the distinguished Roman historian Tacitus, whose *Germania* recounted the failed attempts of the legions of the Roman Empire to subdue the bellicose inhabitants of the land between the Rhine and Oder rivers, defined the Germans as a "distinct, unmixed race, like none but themselves." Several decades earlier, warriors of this singular people had ambushed and defeated a proud, battle-tested force of 20,000 Roman soldiers that made the mistake of leaving the main military highway and venturing into the thick Teutoburger Wald, or Teutoburg Forest (in the present-day *Land*, or state, of North Rhine–Westphalia). Only a handful of the Romans survived to fight another day; the rest were killed in battle, enslaved, tortured to death, or sacrificed to the local gods. Tacitus called the battle frenzy exhibited by the Germans the *furor Teutonicus* (the word *Teutonic* is used to refer to the Germanic peoples) and observed that the Germans were "fanatically loyal to their leaders." Their stamina seemed boundless; according to Tacitus, "Rest is unwelcome to the race." Soon after the Battle of Teutoburger Wald, all the Roman outposts east of the Rhine River save one—Aliso— were overrun. The fortunate defenders of Aliso fled back across the Rhine, and with their retreat serious Roman attempts to subjugate the land it called *Germania barbaria* (barbarian Germany) essentially ended. The Rhine and the Danube rivers, connected by a 300-mile line of fortifications known as the *limes*, came to mark the borders of the Roman Empire, and the fierce Germanic tribes were left to themselves, for the time being.

Barbarians at the Gate

As the Roman Empire weakened under the force of internal and external pressures, the Germanic tribes filled the vacuum left by its demise. Among these were the Franks, the Visigoths, the Ostrogoths, the Lombards, and the Saxons. These barbarians, as the Romans referred to them—the word was used in the ancient world to refer to any non-Roman people—nipped at the flanks of the empire in the east and the west. By the early years of the 5th century, they threatened the city of Rome itself: It was sacked by the Visigoth king Alaric in 410 and by another barbarian leader, Gaiseric, in 455. The German tribes had yet to develop a sense of national identity, however, and they remained divided, unable to fill the void left by the fall of the Roman Empire in the west.

The Carolingian Empire

The Franks eventually emerged as the most powerful German tribe, conquering their rivals and establishing control over territories that stretched from the Pyrenees in the west (the present-day border between Spain and France) to the Oder River in the east, a region that encompassed most of modern France, Germany, the Netherlands, and Belgium as well as a portion of northern Italy. The greatest Frankish king, Karl der Große, known as Charlemagne or Charles the Great, assumed the throne in 768. During his reign, the Carolingian Empire reached its largest extent, and he was instrumental in spreading Christianity among the other

Germanic peoples, such as the conquered Saxons. On Christmas Day in 800, in recognition of his services to a papacy beleaguered by challenges to its authority, Pope Leo III crowned Charlemagne emperor.

The Holy Roman Empire

The coronation of Charlemagne was intended to symbolize the rebirth of the Roman Empire. At its peak, the Roman Empire had extended throughout most of the region along the Mediterranean Sea, into the Middle East and North Africa, and had also included Spain, France (which the Romans called Gaul), and even England. Few of these dominions had failed to be profoundly influenced by Roman civilization and most had benefited, not least through the sense of order that Rome imposed on a tumultuous world. Those subjects who agreed to the *Pax Romana*—the terms of peace that Rome imposed upon its conquered enemies—could at least rest secure in the knowledge that Roman might was pledged to protect them against whatever enemies threatened. Although Rome was always first and foremost a military power, its vassal states could count on enjoying a degree of peace and self-government largely unknown outside the empire, so long as they provided the tribute that Rome demanded.

After the fall of Rome, no power existed that could provide the same sense of order and security in Europe. The term sometimes used to describe the roughly 1,000 years that began with Rome's fall—the Dark Ages—reflects the feeling that Europe then entered a period of decline. In Rome's absence, Christianity became the closest thing to a unifying force. By the time of Charlemagne's coronation, virtually all of Europe had been converted, but just as Rome had been beleaguered by the barbarians, Christianity was challenged by the spread of Islam, the religion established by the prophet Mohammed on the Arabian Peninsula in the 6th century. Islam had spread quickly throughout the Middle East and Africa, and in the 8th century the Moors, North African Muslims, had carried it into Spain. Its advance was halted in 732 at the Battle of Tours, in France, where Charlemagne's grandfather, Charles Martel (Charles the Hammer) defeated a large Moorish force, but in Charlemagne's day it remained firmly established in Spain and also menaced Christian Europe from the east, where it had made inroads on the Balkan Peninsula.

Although most popes of the Middle Ages were of necessity worldly figures very like any of Europe's princes and kings, Christianity was a religious, not a political, doctrine, and the popes exercised their greatest authority in spiritual matters. Because religion was of paramount importance during the Middle Ages and affected virtually every aspect of daily life, this spiritual authority cannot be overestimated. Nevertheless, the popes also saw Christianity as the divinely ordained successor to the Roman Empire and themselves as the head of that empire. They also recognized that their ability to exercise the temporal (worldly, as opposed to spiritual) power to which they aspired was to a large extent dependent upon their ability to maintain the support of the princes and kings who possessed the power to do such extremely useful things as gather funds through taxation and, most important of all, muster armies. It was also clear to the popes that their ability to defend Christianity against such threats as Islam depended upon good relations with the rulers who could put armies in the field.

The coronation of Charlemagne and his later successors thus represented Rome's (in this sense, Rome as the seat of the papacy, not the Roman Empire) attempt to ally itself with what was then the most powerful state in Europe, the Frankish kingdom. Over time this kingdom would give way to the myriad German states loosely united by their nominal fealty to the Roman-coronated emperor, who was often referred to as the *rex Germanorum* (king of the Germans). This union was intended to be mutually beneficial.

Charlemagne's throne sits in the gallery of his palatine chapel at Aachen (Aix-la-Chapelle). Charlemagne's court at Aachen became a center for an artistic and intellectual renaissance—even his octagonal chapel resembles Roman and Byzantine architecture in its design and decoration.

The papacy, the supreme spiritual head of Christianity, thereby availed itself of the military and temporal power of the emperor, who theoretically became, as the great English historian Lord Bryce stated in *The Holy Roman Empire* (published in 1864), the "viceroy of God" and, as one of his titles officially proclaimed, "the Temporal Head of the Faithful." In accepting the crown from the pope, the emperor ostensibly received the sanction of heaven itself for his reign, providing him with legitimacy that could be challenged only at supreme spiritual peril to the challenger. Over time, this singular arrangement between Rome and the German ruler gave rise to the title Holy Roman Empire of the German Nation to describe the German states.

Church vs. State

In practice, the alliance between Rome and the Holy Roman Emperor was an uneasy one, and the countless machinations and intrigues engaged in by the emperors in their unending struggle with the Roman Catholic church helped inspire Voltaire's famous quip that the empire was neither holy, Roman, nor an empire.

The seeds of future discontent were sown early. Charlemagne arranged for his kingdom to be partitioned among his three sons, none of whom was to be crowned emperor. Over the course of the 9th century, the Frankish kingdom came under constant attack from Viking raiders in the north, Saracen marauders from the south, and Magyar horsemen from the east. Weakened even further by quarrels over succession to the throne, the kingdom ultimately broke apart, with the eastern portion, in particular the duchies of Lorraine, Swabia, Bavaria, Saxony, and Franconia, forming the foundation of what would become modern Germany.

Otto I, a Saxon whose achievements would earn him the sobriquet of "the Great," took the throne in 936 and was crowned Holy Roman Emperor in 962. He halted the Magyar advance and decisively defeated the Slavs, thereby adding what was to become Mecklenburg and Brandenburg to the empire and extending its eastern frontier to the Oder River. In 962, Otto responded to the entreaties of Pope John XII, whose unparalleled licentiousness had inspired his enemies to depose him; Otto marched on Rome and restored John to the Holy See. In return, he received concessions from the pope regarding the emperor's control over the church's administration. Almost immediately following Otto's return to Germany, John renounced his promises and allied himself with

Otto's enemies. Otto returned to Rome and summoned a council to depose John, who went into exile. But when the emperor left once more, John regained his authority and wreaked a terrible vengeance upon his opponents. The tradition of struggle between the Holy Roman Emperor (as the secular authority) and the papacy (as the spiritual authority) had been established.

This conflict reached its climax in the 11th century with the battle between the German emperor Heinrich IV and Pope Gregory VII. Gregory, a Benedictine monk who before his election as pope in 1073 had been called Hildebrand, was the leader of a reform movement in the Catholic church that sought to put an end to such practices as the marriage of clergymen, the selling of church offices, and lay *investiture*. (Investiture meant the appointing of bishops and other high church officials.) German princes had long claimed this prerogative for themselves, and Heinrich IV had no intention of surrendering it to the church. The issue involved more than the filling of church offices, for in Germany appointment to a bishopric brought with it a great deal of temporal power as well as spiritual responsibilities. Church officeholders were in essence the administrators for the kingdom, and bishops, for example, were often responsible for collecting taxes and other revenues as well as for the control of the vast church properties. In the words of historian Donald S. Detwiler, the German bishops were not just clergymen but "leading princes of the empire who directly controlled territorial principalities on a level—in terms of political, economic, and military resources—with the most powerful and important German duchies." It is therefore easy to see why the emperor would wish to control who received these appointments, for it was a means by which he could make some of the most influential officials of the realm beholden to him. If the emperor controlled the bishoprics and by extension the thousands of acres of lucrative church lands, he could use his power of patronage to buy, in essence, the loyalty of the princes, dukes, and margraves—the German nobility—who were constantly seeking to extend their privileges at the expense of the monarchy. What made this power doubly attractive was that at the death of a bishop, for example, the lands that he controlled would not be inherited by his heir, as would be the case with noble property, but would revert to the power—church or emperor—invested with the right to dispense them.

Momentum in this struggle was on the side of the church, which in 1059 had succeeded in eliminating the leading role of the emperor in selecting the pope. It should be noted that at this point Germany was still in no sense a formally unified political state but instead a loose collection of entities, united only through the personal influence of the emperor and a vague, inchoate sense of German nationality. The nobility's greatest loyalty was regional, and it was traditionally concerned not so much with some concept of fidelity to a greater German nation as with the protection of its hereditary rights and privileges within the countless duchies, principalities, palatinates, and other political arrangements into which Germany was carved. Heinrich IV therefore regarded the investiture issue as essential, for he recognized that he needed control over the church offices as a bulwark against the power of the nobility.

When Gregory proved unyielding, Heinrich denounced him, questioning his legitimacy as first father of the church and proclaiming him to be not Gregory, the pope, but Hildebrand, a false monk. Declaring that his rights as emperor were invested in him directly by God, not the pope, Heinrich IV challenged Gregory to relinquish the throne of St. Peter—"Come down, come down, and be damned through all the ages!"

Gregory promptly excommunicated Heinrich IV, an action that held considerably more significance than excluding him from the sacraments of the church, for it meant that in the eyes of Rome,

Heinrich IV no longer possessed authority as the Holy Roman Emperor and that his subjects were in no way obligated to fulfill their vows of loyalty to him. The excommunication was tantamount to announcing that Heinrich had been deposed, and the German nobility had no problem in recognizing it as such. Some nobles were moved by opportunism, others by sincere religious motivation, but many saw a chance to diminish the power of the emperor, and rebellion broke out across Germany.

Wasting no time, Gregory set out for Germany to preside over the election of a new emperor. In 1077 a chastened Heinrich IV intercepted him at Canossa, on the northern slopes of the Apen-

In 1077, Heinrich IV appears barefoot in the snow at Canossa to ask for Pope Gregory VII's forgiveness after his excommunication from the church. Although the power struggle between the Holy Roman Emperor and the pope had its roots in the previous century, Heinrich IV and Gregory VII's fight over who would fill bishoprics became the climax of the conflict.

nines; he then knelt barefoot in the snow for three days outside the pope's castle in humble suppliance for the Holy Father's forgiveness. Gregory, a genuinely spiritual man who was later canonized, did not refuse Heinrich IV absolution, but the German nobles were less compassionate and went right ahead with their plan to elect a new, presumably more compliant, king. Years of civil war ensued, to the detriment of the imperial power. In 1122, at Worms, the city where in 1076 Heinrich IV had forced the German bishops to denounce Gregory VII as a false monk, his son and successor, Heinrich V, conceded the right of investiture to the church, retaining only the symbolic power to be present at the investiture ceremony. More important was the change in the balance of power between the king and the nobility, with the nobility gaining at the monarch's expense. The nobles had elected Germany's kings long before Heinrich IV's dispute with Gregory but in doing so had generally observed the principle of hereditary succession. By acting to depose Heinrich IV, Gregory had rejected the notion that any one family ruled by divine right, thereby encouraging the nobles in their growing independence. From that point onward, the nobles would grow ever more zealous in defending their prerogatives and would come to treat the king, in Detwiler's view, as no better than *primus inter pares*—first among equals.

The Two Friedrichs

Following the death of Heinrich V, the division among the German nobility grew more pronounced, and Germany was racked by civil war. The two predominant parties were the Saxons and Bavarians, known jointly as the Guelphs (the word is derived from the Italian translation of the name of one of the leading Bavarian families, the Welfs), who supported the authority and independence of the papacy; and the Franconian and Swabian supporters of the imperial house of Hohenstaufen, known jointly as the Ghibellines (from the Italian name for the city of Waiblingen, where many of their most important princes were born), who supported the power of the Holy Roman Emperor at the expense of the papacy. The Guelphs were also supported by the many Italian city-states that no longer wished to be beholden to a German emperor.

After the death of Heinrich V, Germany was torn apart by the squabbling between the noble factions, each of whom supported their own candidate for the throne, the Ghibellines by virtue of election, the Guelphs by virtue of heredity. The disorder in the kingdom grew so pronounced that in 1152 both sides, exhausted, were able to agree on the accession of Friedrich I, a Hohenstaufen closely related to the Guelphs through his mother. Often referred to as Barbarossa (Redbeard), which is what the Italians called him, Friedrich restored peace to Germany and added much of northern Italy, Burgundy, and Bohemia to its dominions. His triumph over his great rival, Heinrich, called Henry the Lion, duke of Saxony and Bavaria—whom he stripped of his feudal lands—was finally achieved through use of the courts rather than an exercise of absolute royal power, a course of action that helped bind Germany's nobles more closely to him. It was during Barbarossa's 38-year reign that the term Holy Roman Empire came into popular usage. One of the most beloved German kings, Friedrich was killed in 1190 while leading a force of 20,000 knights to the Holy Land on the Third Crusade, apparently when he fell from his horse and drowned in a stream. According to German legend, however, he did not die but waits, asleep, in a secret cave deep inside the mountain ridge of the Kyffhäuser, for the moment when he will awaken and restore the empire to its past glory.

Barbarossa's extremely ambitious son, Heinrich VI, concerned himself mainly with increasing the power of the empire in southern Italy. He led no less than six separate military expeditions to Italy and succeeded in having himself crowned king of The Two Sicilies (a kingdom that included the island of Sicily and much of southern Italy), but this was achieved at the expense of a certain neglect of affairs in Germany, where succession quarrels involving the fractious nobility resumed after his death from malaria, at the tender age of 32, in 1197.

Once again Germany descended into civil war between the Guelphs, who held Otto of Brunswick, the son of Henry the Lion, to be the rightful emperor, and the Ghibellines, who supported the candidacy of Philip of Swabia, the brother of Heinrich VI. Otto ultimately won, becoming the only Guelph emperor, but he over-reached himself when he attacked lands the pope claimed as his own. With help from the French, the Ghibellines routed Otto at the Battle of Bouvines in the summer of 1214, and Friedrich II, the grandson of Friedrich Barbarossa, took the throne.

Called by philosopher Friedrich Nietzsche the first European, by his contemporaries *stupor mundi* (the marvel of the world), and by many historians the first modern monarch, Friedrich II was destined to be revered as one of Germany's greatest rulers. Yet, like his uncle Heinrich VI, he was much more concerned with his southern than his northern holdings. In his 35-year reign, which lasted from 1215 to 1250, he visited Germany only 3 times—once for his coronation and then only for a couple of months on 2 other occasions. A poet and scientist, Friedrich II achieved the most in Sicily, his birthplace, where he enacted a number of significant reforms, chief among them the establishment of an efficient, honest, and highly trained government bureaucracy. In 1228, in fulfillment of a vow he had made to the pope, Friedrich II succeeded, through diplomacy backed by the threat of military might, in freeing Jerusalem from the Muslims. Thereafter, however, he continued his predecessors' assaults against Italy, and the papacy came to regard him as a scourge. Nevertheless, during his reign, both the church and the nobility gained in power in Germany. Friedrich II exempted Germany's bishops and other churchmen from the last remnants of lay control, and in the course of reforming the structure of Germany's government, he granted the land's princes increased autonomy over the legislative process, the judiciary, taxes and monetary policy, and the control of roads and byways. At his death in 1250, the medieval German empire had achieved its greatest geographic extent, stretching west to east from the Scheldt and Rhône rivers to beyond the Oder, and from the Baltic and North seas in the north to Italy in the south, where it encompassed all but the Papal States in the center and the northeastern portion of the peninsula.

Albrecht Dürer's engraving Knight, Death, and the Devil *(1513) combines Germanic and Italian Renaissance themes: The Christian knight, who is accompanied by a dog that symbolizes the virtues of untiring zeal, learning, and truth, rides steadfastly toward his destiny, ignoring the figures of Death, on his right, and the Devil, behind him.*

3

The Center Cannot Hold

Germany's great size made it a formidable power, but it also made it extremely difficult to govern. This problem was aggravated by the continuing fragmentation of power in the realm. The death of Friedrich II brought on a new interregnum in which various candidates and their supporting factions struggled for the throne. France, which had begun to fear the potential might of its eastern neighbor, and the papacy collaborated with the German nobles in limiting the power of the emperor. In general, those who succeeded in attaining the German throne at this time concerned themselves more with solidifying their power in their hereditary duchies and principalities than with increasing the strength of the monarchy over Germany as a whole. Although the Golden Bull of 1356 formalized the procedure for electing the Holy Roman Emperor by eliminating the role of the papacy and designating seven electors—the archbishops of Mainz, Cologne, and Trier, the duke of Saxony, the king of Bohemia, the count palatine of the Rhine, and the margrave of Brandenburg; more were added later—this only increased the power of the nobility, for the electors were granted quasi-royal privileges in their respective regions.

As a result, by the mid-14th century, Germany was a collection of literally hundreds of different political entities, ranging in size from larger kingdoms and principalities, such as Bavaria and Brandenburg, to independent cities to tiny baronies that were the minute holdings of thousands of individual free knights, the descendants of a warrior class that owed its loyalty only to the emperor. The steady rise of a merchant class, which of necessity valued stability and coherence in the empire as conducive to the orderly conduct of business, gave rise to new political and economic organizations designed to provide merchants and traders with the protection that might otherwise have been the responsibility of a strong central government. The most significant of these were the various alliances formed by the cities of western and southern Germany against the privations of the knights, whose practice of extorting outrageous toll and highway fees for the use of roads passing through their holdings was particularly damaging to business. The knights formed their own organizations—the leagues of St. George, of St. William, and of the Lion, for example—and the cities and the knights often warred. The other important urban alliance was the Hanseatic League, which was organized by the seafaring merchant towns of northern Germany to protect them against foreign competition and piracy. Bremen, Hamburg, and Lübeck were the most important Hanseatic cities, but in contrast with England and France, where the cities of London and Paris were already becoming truly national metropolises, urban development in Germany mirrored its political fragmentation. A great number of comparatively small cities attained considerable regional significance as economic and cultural centers, but no single city played a dominant role in national affairs. An equally important development that occurred at about this time was the *Drang nach Osten* (drive toward the east), as the eastward migration that nearly doubled the extent of German-inhabited territory was known. By the 14th century, western Germany was heavily populated, and the amount of land available to the peasantry was consequently small. Thus, German peasants were more than willing to settle and develop sparsely populated regions in Austria, Hungary, Bohemia, and Poland.

Despite its political unwieldiness, Germany was both economically and culturally prosperous as the Middle Ages gave way to the Renaissance. Its cities and merchants were well off, and in such cities as Freiburg, Cologne, and Strasbourg the construction of magnificent Gothic cathedrals testified to the vitality of the church. In 1455, in the city of Mainz, a printer named Johannes Gutenberg produced the first book made from movable type, the Bible. Although Gutenberg was forced to sell his famous printing press because of indebtedness, his invention remains one of the most important technological innovations of all ages, because it made possible for the first time the mass production and widespread dissemination of the written word. (In fact, Germany today is a leading exporter of printing and papermaking machines.) Perhaps the strongest evidence of Germany's cultural achievements during this period, however, is the work of its four greatest painters.

Firmly Fixed

Little is known for certain about the artist who survives in history as Matthias Grünewald except for the undeniable power of his masterpieces. It is probable that even the name by which he has come down through the ages is a misnomer; more likely the painter renowned for his stark portrayal of the pain and terror endured by Christ on the Cross at Calvary was born Mathis Gothart Neithart. Grünewald left behind no explanations of his artistic theory, but it is clear that he was uninfluenced by the notions of classical beauty that informed the Italian Renaissance, for he emphasized color and the effects of darkness and light at the expense of anatomical correctness. His greatest work was the

Isenheim Altarpiece, completed in 1515. The central panel of the exterior of the altarpiece, the Crucifixion, is an almost unbearable depiction of Christ's agony. The *Isenheim Altarpiece* was painted for the commandery, or district manor, of the Hospital Order of St. Anthony and was seen by the sufferers of the many diseases treated by the hospital order. Grünewald's Savior is clearly human and has suffered the mortification of torture and a horrible death, but in the work's accompanying panel, the Resurrection, he rises anew, in the full vigor of salvation and clothed in a radiant light. Christ's resurrection is portrayed here as a cataclysm that sweeps the prostrate Roman soldiers and the rocks of the Savior's tomb

Matthias Grünewald's central Crucifixion panel of the Isenheim Altarpiece *(1515) depicts the agony of Christ's tortured death. Grünewald has often been called the last medieval mystic because of his preoccupation with suffering and his vision of a battered world.*

away into the darkness, far from the brilliant halo of the new life. Such is the force of faith in the world, Grünewald clearly says, and like Christ, the sick at the hospital could also be freed of their pain and suffering.

The work of Grünewald's contemporary, Lucas Cranach the Elder, is much less powerful, but it too makes use of brilliant color rather than classical composition to create its effects. In 1505, Cranach became the court painter to Frederick the Wise of Saxony in Wittenberg. Cranach painted a diversity of subjects, including the female nude, mythological and allegorical scenes, and religious works. He painted half-length portraits naturalistically, presenting the figures close to the picture plane, using dramatic landscape as background, and combining a northern accentuation on atmosphere and variety of texture with rich, warm color. Some art historians criticize as superficial Cranach's later work, which was done after he became a sort of court painter for Martin Luther and is more concerned with portraiture, mythology, and history than with overt religious themes. However, Cranach's realistic treatment of nature as encountered in the foothills of the German Alps heralded the development of landscape painting and influenced the type of painting—embraced by the so-called Danube School of artists, including Albrecht Altdorfer—which was characterized by its emphasis on nature rather than figures and objects.

Born in the city of Augsburg in 1497 and settling in Basel around 1514, Hans Holbein the Younger was of a later generation than Grünewald or Cranach. (He was 22 years younger than the former, 25 years younger than the latter.) Perhaps for that reason—the ideas of such masters of the late Italian Renaissance as Leonardo da Vinci, Michelangelo, and Raphael had had more time to filter into Germany—his great early works, such as *The Madonna of Burgomaster Meyer*, completed in 1528, reflect the influence of both the Italian and the northern schools of painting. The Italian emphasis on harmonious composition—that is, the placement of the

Hans Holbein the Younger completed the painting Madonna of Burgomaster Meyer *in 1528; he monumentalized his composition by changing the scale of the figures. Holbein found that there was more opportunity for painting portraiture in England than in Basel and left for London in 1532. He later became court painter for King Henry VIII.*

figures in the painting to achieve a sense of balance and order—is evident in the symmetrical arrangement of the kneeling Meyer family on either side of the standing Virgin Mary, whereas the northern influence can be seen in Holbein's carefully detailed presentation of the contemporary clothing worn by his subjects and in his insistence on a realistic depiction of their facial features, which is much closer to portraiture than the idealized conception of beauty of the Italian masters. Driven from Basel by the religious conflicts that wracked the region through much of the 16th century, Holbein wound up as the court painter of Henry VIII of England; his seemingly simple portraits, characterized by scrupulous fidelity to detail, reveal considerable insight into the character of his sitters. His masterpieces of portraiture include *Erasmus of Rotterdam, Archbishop Warham, Sir Thomas More,* and many paintings of Henry VIII.

If achievement is built on ambition, it is only fitting that Albrecht Dürer (1471–1528), painter, printmaker, and theoretician, should enjoy the high reputation he has claimed for nearly five centuries, for more than any other German artist of the time, Dürer felt keenly what he regarded as the artistic inferiority of the north in comparison with wondrous Italy, and he labored intensely all his life to capture the artistic fire of the Italian geniuses. In 1505, when he left Nuremberg and was received warmly in the Italian city of Venice, the home of his revered masters Titian, Tintoretto, and especially Giovanni Bellini, he exulted. "How I shall shiver for the sun," he wrote in a letter to a friend in Germany. "Here I am a lord, at home a parasite." Yet Dürer's protestations of hostility and indifference on the part of his countrymen ring a distinctly false note, particularly in contrast with the truthfulness of his art. Dürer was Germany's first artistic celebrity, no less lauded in his homeland than he was in Italy and elsewhere on the continent.

For all his admiration of the painters of the south, Dürer is quintessentially a northern artist in that his particular genius most reveals itself in works that reflect his careful observation and detailed re-creation of the natural and material world. Where the Italians strove to represent spiritual truths and to create an ideal conception of beauty (that "certain idea" of beauty that Raphael, for example, held in his mind), Dürer, in watercolors such as *The Hare* and *The Great Piece of Turf*, achieved instead an almost photographically precise depiction of nature. Dürer regarded "a form and figure out of nature with more pleasure than any other, though the thing itself is not necessarily altogether better or worse." For him, nature and beauty were inseparable. "Depart not from nature in your opinions," he advised other artists, "neither imagine that you can invent anything better . . . for art stands firmly fixed in nature, and he who can find it there, he has it." In his woodcuts and engravings, which because they were widely circulated at prices that ordinary people could afford were even

Dürer's watercolor The Hare *(1502) displays the artist's curiosity about nature and his concern with detail; in Dürer's hands, the hare, a small part of nature, becomes a work of art.*

more responsible for his popularity in Germany than his paintings, Dürer showed a similar concern with realistic depiction of detail. The stable in his engraving *Nativity*, completed in 1504, is a tottering, crumbling edifice on its way back to nature; trees grow from a broken outer wall and birds nest atop the loose broken boards that serve it as a roof. Dürer portrayed each crack and chink in the humble structure with careful detail; almost unnoticed, in a rude shed at the lower left, Mary and a shepherd pray over the newborn Christ child. On the surface, there is little of the splendor and magnificence with which a southern artist might have invested a nativity scene, yet a sense of wonder still prevails. Dürer's method reinforces the spiritual content of his message: Amid the modest and timeworn things of this world miracles are born.

The Habsburgs

In 1438, Albert II, a member of the Habsburg family, the ruling house of Austria, was crowned Holy Roman Emperor. Except for two brief interregnums, the Habsburgs would rule the empire until Napoléon Bonaparte dissolved it in 1806. Maximilian I, who ruled from 1493 to 1519, was known as the Last Knight because he was courageous, chivalrous, and a great patron of the arts—Dürer was his court painter. As a result of a series of marital alliances inspired by Maximilian, when Charles V (Karl V, Maximilian I's grandson), the last Holy Roman Emperor to be crowned by a pope, took the throne in 1519, he ruled not only the German-speaking lands but Spain, the Netherlands, and much of Italy.

Somber, diligent, and extremely religious, Charles V may have been the most powerful monarch in Europe, the holder of 75 titles, and the ruler of an empire over which, he said, "the sun never set," but he was unable to achieve centralization of power in Germany. Born and raised in the Netherlands, king of Spain three years before he became Holy Roman Emperor, Charles spent only brief periods in Germany during his lifetime. Larger strategic questions concerned him more than did German reform; he regarded the continued loyalty of the plethora of German principalities to the Habsburgs as being more important than their ability to act in concert in accordance with some notion of German nationhood. Furthermore, when Charles V came to the throne, Germany was being rent by a spiritual schism that would ultimately divide all of Europe.

The Reformation

On October 31, 1517, a 34-year-old priest and professor of biblical studies at the University of Wittenberg named Martin Luther nailed a document, written in Latin, to the door of the castle church in Wittenberg. The document eloquently detailed, in 95 separate points, its author's disagreements with current church practice and doctrine. Widely disseminated by like-minded reformers and scholars, Luther's Ninety-five Theses ignited a religious conflagration that soon engulfed most of the continent.

Luther's chief objection was to the church doctrine of salvation through works, which held that the eternal life of the spirit could be won through moral actions. Over time, this concept had been corrupted to include in meaning and practice the sale of indulgences—literally, papal certificates of redemption for sins. Indulgences were obtained by performing specific devotions, usually to holy relics obtained by princes and church fathers, and by donating prescribed amounts of money. A certain donation bought one, for example, a reduction in the amount of time a soul might otherwise have to spend in purgatory before ascending to heaven. The sale of indulgences preyed upon the piety and fears of the faithful while greatly increasing the power, prestige, and wealth of churchmen.

This practice had been widespread for centuries and had been decried nearly as long, but Luther's protest was timely for several reasons. In the previous decades, the sale of indulgences had reached new heights. Between 1509 and 1520 Luther's own prince—the elector of Saxony, Frederick the Wise—increased his

Martin Luther was a priest and a professor of theology at the University of Wittenberg when he nailed his Ninety-five Theses to the Wittenberg church door in 1517. Luther's list of points attacking the Roman Catholic church's practice of selling indulgences caused a considerable scandal in Germany and led to what is now called the Reformation.

stock of sacred relics from 5,000 to 19,013. These, according to the catalogs he circulated, included a thorn from the crown of thorns worn by Jesus on the cross, a nail that had held him there, a twig from the burning bush of Moses, and four strands of the Virgin Mary's hair. Purchasers of indulgences from Frederick the Wise could obtain remittances of their terms in purgatory of 1,902,202 years and 27 days. The elector used the revenues from the sale of indulgences for, among other things, the operation and improvement of the University of Wittenberg.

Even better bargains were available elsewhere for the shopper eager to ensure favorable future treatment for his or her soul. In 1517, sales agents for the Great Indulgence offered by Pope Leo X fanned out across Germany. The pontiff was in a great hurry to raise funds to finish the construction of St. Peter's Basilica in Rome, and his indulgence promised great dividends. Not only could the purchaser obtain a papal passport to heaven but for an additional fee, retroactive indulgences could be obtained for friends and relatives who had already died and might be suffering the stings of purgatory. A popular rhyme of the day reflected the alleged efficacy of Leo's Great Indulgence:

As soon as the money in the box rings
The soul from purgatory's fire springs

Although Frederick the Wise banned Leo's salesmen from Saxony, it was Leo's indulgence, and in particular the manual of instructions the archbishop of Mainz had prepared for the pope's salesmen, that inspired Luther's wrath. Luther followed his theses with a barrage of pamphlets and dissertations that attacked the corruption of the church, specifically the doctrine of works and the sale of indulgences. He argued that faith alone was sufficient for a person to attain salvation, and he emphasized individual interpretation of the Scriptures. When the pope demanded that Luther recant his accusations, Luther refused and was excommunicated in 1521. Despite calls from church bodies for his seizure and imprisonment, Luther remained safe under the protection of Frederick the Wise.

Following Luther's excommunication, his movement gradually evolved from a quest to reform the Catholic church to the creation of a new, separate, reformed church. The printing press permitted the mass circulation of the unending stream of circulars and broadsides penned by Luther—he published an average of one a month until his death in 1546—and he quickly acquired a wide following. More important, he succeeded in winning the support of a large number of the German princes. Some were motivated by genuine religious conviction, others by the realization that Luther's movement offered the opportunity to create a specifically German church that would bring with its foundation a great reduction in the power of the papacy and Catholic church officials in Germany and a corresponding increase in their own might. For example, Frederick the Wise protected Luther not out of any innate sympathy for his ideas but because he resented the attempts of Rome to dictate the teachings of a professor at his university. Likewise, Frederick had banned the salesmen of the Great Indulgence from his realm not because he opposed indulgences—his coffers were filled with gold florins obtained from their sale—but because he did not want the money usually spent by purchasers in Saxony to go to Rome. Other German princes seized upon the Reformation movement as a pretext to confiscate church lands and break the power of the bishops. Thousands of private citizens were drawn to Lutheranism by the notion of personal freedom seemingly inherent in Luther's espousal of the individual relationship between each human and God, which many interpreted as having profound political ramifications in terms of the relationship between government and the governed. Many believed as well that the overthrow of the spiritual authority of the church heralded a revolution in the relations between master and man. For the most

Pope Leo X, here depicted in a painting by Raphael, was a great patron of the arts, and his reign exemplified the luxury and magnificence of the papacy during the Renaissance. Although he tried, unsuccessfully, to reform the church at the Fifth Lateran Council in Rome, his most famous act was the excommunication of Martin Luther on January 3, 1521.

part, Luther did not share these interpretations and faithfully upheld the authority of the princes. For example, when Germany was convulsed in the mid-1520s by the so-called Peasants' War, in which thousands of peasants, citing Luther as among their inspirations, rose up to shake off the oppression of the nobility, which owned most of Germany's land, Luther responded with a pamphlet, *Against Robbing and Murdering Gangs of Peasants*, that encouraged the princes to be ruthless in crushing the uprisings. You must "smite, strangle, and stab," Luther advised his princely supporters. "It is just as when you must kill a mad dog; if you don't get him, he will kill you."

The staunchly Catholic Charles V initially sought to dismiss the tumult unleashed by Luther as nothing more than a "monks' quarrel," but it more closely resembled a civil war; and by the middle of the 16th century a little more than half of Germany had proclaimed itself Lutheran or one of Lutheranism's Protestant offshoots. In general, the strongest Protestant regions were in the north of Germany, the most ardently Catholic in the south. By virtue of the Peace of Augsburg of 1555, an uneasy truce between the Protestants and the Catholics prevailed—*Cuius regio, eius religio* (In his own realm, his own religion), whereby each prince determined the religious faith of his own people—and the fighting in Germany was halted for several decades.

Luther's Bible

Luther's significance as a literary figure in German history is almost as important as his achievements as a religious reformer, although these two aspects of his life's work cannot really be separated, as they are but opposite sides of the same coin. As the reader has seen, part of the reason that the Reformation spread so quickly and widely was Luther's skill as a writer, his tirelessness as a polemicist, and the availabilty of new technology that made it easy to disseminate his teachings. Central to Luther's thought was the notion that the Bible must be made available to everyone so that each person could come to an individual knowledge and understanding of the Scriptures. Luther saw that because Catholic masses were said in Latin and the Bible was available only in Latin, the word of God was therefore only directly accessible to the most educated members of society—in Germany at the time, a small, elite segment indeed. Most of the people therefore were dependent upon priests for their religious understanding. Luther wanted to change this; the great reformer of Wittenberg believed that the Gospels and the Old Testament should be available to everyone. Accordingly, much of his time and energy was devoted to preparing a German translation of the Bible. Luther's Bible is considered the absolute masterpiece of German prose; its appearance also did more than any other single document to standardize the German language. Its significance in German literature is equivalent to that of the King James Bible in English in that, if only for the sheer beauty and majesty of their language, both are regarded as the supreme evocation in their tongue of the holy truths of the Judeo-Christian tradition.

The Thirty Years' War

The Counter-Reformation, as Catholic Europe's response to the challenge of Protestantism was known, culminated in the carnage and catastrophe of the Thirty Years' War. The war began in about 1618 as a continuation of the ongoing struggle in Germany between the Catholic and Protestant princes, but it soon grew into a larger conflict that brought several of Europe's strongest powers—Protestant England and Sweden, Catholic France—into league with the German Protestants in an effort to limit, if not break, the power of the Habsburg Holy Roman Empire. The war began over the attempts of the Bohemian nobles to overthrow their realm's Catholic king; when the Habsburg forces, through the inspired leadership of such generals as Johann von Tilly and Albrecht von Wallenstein, proved triumphant in the war's early phases, Denmark, and more important, powerful Sweden, entered on the Protestant side. More years of bloodshed followed, until the exhausted combatants agreed upon a peace at Prague in 1635. But for years France had been wary of the increasing power of the Habsburgs, and its chief government minister, the wily and nefarious Cardinal Richelieu, now recognized a prime opportunity to strike against his nemesis. France was fervently Catholic, but Richelieu, a master of *realpolitik* (politics based on practical and material factors), if ever there was one, nevertheless made common cause with the Swedes and the German Protestant princes. The bloodiest phase of the war then ensued, with Spanish forces joining the Habsburg troops and England aiding the anti-imperialist armies until the Treaty of Westphalia ended the war in 1648. The Habsburgs still ruled, but Germany, where virtually all of the fighting had taken place, was prostrate, demolished physically, economically, and spiritually.

It is virtually impossible to overestimate the significance of the Thirty Years' War in relation to Germany's national development. The devastation endured by Germany was truly shattering. The *Soldateska* (soldiers) unleashed upon Germany by their commanders were infamous for their brutality and rapacity. Looting, rape, arson, and other atrocities, directed against civilians as well as combatants, were commonplace. Entire towns were leveled; crops were burned and the countryside was laid waste. Neither side was virtuous in its conduct of the war. In one notable episode, the troops commanded by Tilly, who was known as the Monk in Armor because of his blameless personal life, ran amok on the citizens of Magdeburg, a Protestant town on the Elbe River. When the smoke cleared and the carnage ceased, only 5,000 of the town's 30,000 inhabitants were left alive. Such incidents were the rule rather than the exception. According to historian Gordon Craig, in the last 18 years of the war, Swedish troops alone destroyed 18,000 villages, 1,500 towns, and 200 castles. In one of the great works of German literature from about this time, Hans Jakob Christoffel von Grimmelshausen's picaresque novel *Der Abentheuerliche Simplicissimus* (The Adventurous Simplicissimus), the protagonist tags along with a group of plundering soldiers who "swept through the villages, stole and took what they wanted, mocked and ruined the peasants and violated their maids and wives and daughters and, if the poor peasants didn't like that and dared to be brave and to rap one or the other forager across the knuckles because of their deeds, then one cut them down, if one could catch them, or at least sent their houses up to heaven in smoke." Starvation in the countryside was rampant; in some areas the unfortunate peasants resorted to cannibalism to survive. In Württemberg, the population was reduced from 400,000 to 48,000; Bohemia's populace dwindled from 3 million to 780,000, and at war's end only 5,000 of its 35,000 villages still stood. Overall, the population of Germany dropped from 21 million to 13 million. Germany's economic devastation corresponded to its human loss, and the damage to the nation's collective spiritual and psychological well-being is simply impossible to estimate. It took generations for Germany to recover.

Politically, the consequences for Germany of the Thirty Years' War were almost as great. The anti-imperialist forces had not succeeded in crushing the Habsburgs, but as a result of the Peace of Westphalia, which was proclaimed on October 24, 1648, France emerged as the war's true winner. Recognizing that Germany's continued political fragmentation was of benefit because it prevented Germany from acting as a united power, France established itself as a guarantor of the sovereignty of the individual German states, which after the Peace of Westphalia numbered more than 300. For centuries to come, the rest of Europe regarded German disunity as integral to the balance of power on the continent. In the Peace of Westphalia, Germany was also deprived of control over all its river outlets to the sea. Poland controlled much of the Baltic coastline, Sweden claimed the Oder River and surrounding territory, Denmark governed the right bank of the Elbe, and the Netherlands—whose independence was at last formally recognized—watched over the mouth of the Rhine. At a time when the other European powers, most notably Spain, France, and England, were in the process of developing new trade routes and consolidating vast colonial empires overseas, Germany found itself essentially landlocked.

Friedrich II, called Frederick the Great, (rear center) and the French writer Voltaire (facing Friedrich at left) were good friends; in fact, in 1750, Voltaire came to live at Sans Souci, the king's palace near Potsdam, at Friedrich's request. Friedrich was often called the philosopher-king because he was an intellectual as well as a prolific writer on political matters.

4

The Obedient Land

In the aftermath of the Thirty Years' War, the power of the German princes and nobility increased. The war left the peasantry and middle class devastated, and in the countryside the nobility was able to increase its landholdings at the expense of the lower classes. In most of the German states, the government became highly bureaucratized. Most of these high officials were prominent nobles; below them were educated members of the upper class. There was little opportunity for popular participation in political life; all were beholden to the ruling prince. German society, as countless historians and other observers have remarked upon, became characterized by an extremely high degree of loyalty and obedience to the ruling class. This was not a new phenomenon— one of the popes of the Middle Ages had described Germany as the *terra obedientiae* (Latin for the obedient land)—but in the 17th and 18th centuries it intensified. The greatest catalyst for this change was the national cataclysm Germany had recently endured. In the war's wake, Germans seemed willing to give unquestioning obedience to strong government because it promised the greatest protection against the kind of devastation that they had recently experienced. Over time, obedience and loyalty to government acquired the weight of tradition, cloaked itself in the sanctity of virtue, and became a national characteristic much commented on by outside and German observers alike. Karl Friedrich Moser, a famous German publisher of the Enlightenment, wrote in 1758: "Every nation has its principal motive. In Germany it is obedience; in England, freedom; in Holland, trade; in France, the honor of the King."

Despite its continuing political fragmentation, a new emphasis on the uniqueness and value of things German became evident at about this same time. This trend was particularly pronounced in the so-called German heartland, the region of mid-sized towns and cities set in the countryside that stretched from Westphalia to the Danube and from the Rhine to upper Saxony. This area, as contrasted with Austria and Bavaria to the south and Prussia to the north, was viewed by its inhabitants as the repository of the German essence. Writing in 1865, the great German composer Richard Wagner, who was obsessed with the idea of German identity and whose operas made potent use of German mythology and symbolism, noted: "After the complete destruction of the German essence, after the almost complete extinction of the German nation as a result of the indescribable devastations of the Thirty Years' War, it was this most intimately homely world from which the German spirit was reborn."

The Rise of Prussia

To its European neighbors, this German resurgence took the form of a preoccupation with military concerns, as illustrated by the rise of Prussia, the electorate and then kingdom (from 1701) of northeast Germany that at its greatest territorial extent would constitute two-thirds of the German nation. Prussia's ascension began during the 48-year reign of Friedrich Wilhelm, the Great Elector and the first of the great rulers of the house of Hohenzollern, who

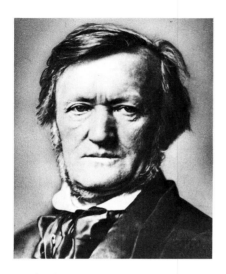

The composer Richard Wagner revolutionized romantic opera in Germany during the second half of the 19th century. He often used German mythology as a basis for his librettos and combined German legends with impassioned romantic music to create highly theatrical operas, including Lohengrin, Tristan und Isolde, *and* Der Ring des Nibelungen.

took the throne as the elector of Brandenburg in 1640. Friedrich Wilhelm succeeded, through force of arms, in reclaiming much of his state from Sweden, which had occupied it during the Thirty Years' War. In 1660, he brought Prussia under his rule. His son, Friedrich I, crowned himself king of Prussia in 1701 and continued the policy of territorial expansion begun by his father, but his achievements paled in comparison with those of his son and successor, Friedrich Wilhelm I, who during his reign, which lasted from 1713 to 1740, increased the Prussian army from 40,000 to 83,000 troops. This gave Prussia the fourth-largest army in Europe, despite its being only 10th in size and 13th in population.

Friedrich II (1740–86)

Friedrich Wilhelm I's army, the pride of Prussia, was inherited and put to use by his son, Friedrich II, known as Frederick the Great. A bookish and somewhat timid child who was easily intimidated by his verbally and physically abusive father, Friedrich II was initially reluctant to inherit the throne and even attempted to escape Prussia, but he was captured and then forced to witness the beheading of his best friend, who had aided him in his plans to flee. After that,

Friedrich II never again attempted to shirk his hereditary obligations. An extremely cultured and refined individual, he befriended and supported the French writer Voltaire, wrote passable poetry, became an accomplished musician, and penned superb essays that attempted to refute the political philosophy of Machiavelli, but as a ruler he was an uncompromising practitioner of power politics whose wars added great expanses of territory to Prussia. At the same time, he instituted a series of sweeping economic and legal reforms that made Prussia one of the most modern and best-governed states of Europe. His victories in the War of the Austrian Succession (1740–48) and the Seven Years' War (1756–63) made Prussia the most feared military power in Europe and left his state and Austria—which was still ruled by his great enemies, the Habsburgs—on a collision course regarding German supremacy.

Napoléon Bonaparte

Despite all his services for Prussia, Friedrich II was an avid Francophile, an admirer of the literature, music, philosophy, art, and especially the language of France, in which his own excellent prose was written. Friedrich II even went so far as to pronounce German culture "vulgar." In the latter half of the 18th century, this admiration for France was shared by many German intellectuals. France was then the center of the intellectual movement known as the Enlightenment, which emphasized the role of reason in ordering and governing human affairs. Voltaire, Friedrich's great friend, was perhaps the most important literary figure in Enlightenment France; Friedrich II, with his domestic emphasis on progress and the rule of law, was the quintessential Enlightenment despot.

Many Enlightenment thinkers, in France and elsewhere, championed democracy; thus, the rise of Napoléon Bonaparte to power in France following the revolution that overthrew the royal family was welcomed by a sizable segment of the German population, who believed that Napoléon would bring democracy to the rest of Europe. Support for Napoléon in Germany was strongest among the intellectuals and those princes who resented the power of the Habsburgs and Prussia. Conversely, Austria and Prussia were among the European states that regarded the French Revolution in general and Napoléon in particular as a diabolical threat to the established order. Both fought against Napoléon's vaunted Grande Armée, which by 1810 had swept over much of Europe, but it was not until Bonaparte overextended himself by invading Russia in 1812 that they were able to make any headway against him. By that point, Napoléon had annexed all of Germany west of the Rhine, abolished the Holy Roman Empire (in 1806), and established in its place the Confederation of the Rhine (Württemberg, Bavaria, Saxony, Westphalia, and 32 smaller principalities that Napoléon had consolidated out of the dozens of German states) under his control.

Following Napoléon's final defeat at Waterloo and permanent exile to St. Helena in 1815, the European nations met at the Austrian city of Vienna to construct a new balance of power for Europe. Both Austria and Prussia (two of the four major powers at the meeting, which also included Russia and Britain) argued against the unification of Germany, which some diplomats favored as a means of holding France in check. Both cited the traditional liberties of the German states as the reason for their opposition, but both were equally moved by their own reluctance to see this theoretical German state dominated by the other. Instead, the diplomats, under the guidance of the Austrian statesman and prince Klemens von Metternich, established the German Confederation, an extremely loose union of the 39 German states (including the four free cities of Hamburg, Bremen, Lübeck, and Frankfurt), each of which was represented in a legislative body known as the Diet. Austria was awarded the permanent chairmanship of the Diet, which was to meet at Frankfurt; Prussia was stripped of much of the territory it had carved away from Poland but was rewarded for its role in defeating Napoléon with much of Saxony and sizable chunks of the Rhineland and Westphalia as well.

In ending Napoléon's 20-year dominance of the Continent (only the Scandinavian nations were not visited by his armies), the diplomats at Vienna tried to restore the old order in Europe, placing the heirs to the hereditary ruling dynasties in France and Spain back on their thrones. In Germany, however, despite the changes wrought by Napoléon, the old order had remained essentially intact.

A Flowering of German Culture

Ironically, as Germany faced the possibility of political extinction during the Napoleonic era, its writers and composers were enhancing its cultural prestige to the extent that the German city of Weimar threatened to outshine Paris, Europe's intellectual capital. It was during this period that the literary powers of the poet, dramatist, and novelist Johann Wolfgang von Goethe and the playwright Friedrich von Schiller, Goethe's close friend, reached

The composer Ludwig van Beethoven (1770–1827) demonstrated that music could be a means of personal expression. He was often described as "half-crazy" because of his oddness, and after he became deaf he was looked upon by many as a tormented musical genius.

their peak. Schiller's greatest play, *Wallenstein*, about the general of the same name from the Thirty Years' War, appeared in 1799, while between 1796 and 1809 Goethe produced his great character study, *The Apprenticeship of Wilhelm Meister*, his psychological novel *Elective Affinities*, and the first part of his epic poem *Faust*. Goethe's earlier novel, *The Sorrows of Young Werther*, the story of a lovesick swain who commits suicide after he is rebuffed by his beloved, heralded much of the sensibility of the German Romantic movement.

The presence of Goethe and Schiller made the city of Weimar the literary capital of Germany, if not of all Europe. Among the other influential German writers who spent time in Weimar were the poet Friedrich Hölderlin and the master of the short story Heinrich von Kleist. The importance of their work aside, their life could have served as inspiration for the German literature of the day, with its emphasis on individual sensibility, heroism, and tragedy. Like characters from a German Romantic poem or novel, both were highly sensitive persons who believed themselves to be greatly misunderstood and who suffered for the sake of their art. Both were also highly individualistic, idiosyncratic writers whose reputation in the 20th century has outshone that which they enjoyed in their own day; both were figures of tragedy whose misfortune curtailed their literary production. Kleist committed suicide at a young age; Hölderlin spent the last 37 years of his life hopelessly insane.

Among the other artistic giants who came to Weimar was the composer Ludwig van Beethoven. Beethoven's great Third Symphony—his favorite symphony, known popularly as the Eroica—was dedicated to Napoléon until the composer, an ardent republican, learned that the Frenchman had proclaimed himself emperor. "Now he too will trample on the rights of man, and indulge only his own ambition," Beethoven thundered as he scratched out the dedication on the title page, his pen raking a hole in the score. A great admirer of Goethe's, Beethoven wrote songs based on several of the writer's poems and composed music for his play *Egmont*. Their characters were incompatible, however; Goethe preferred to maintain a polished, Olympian aloofness, whereas Beethoven was something of an enfant terrible, passionate and unconcerned with the etiquette of high society. Goethe wrote of him, "His talent amazed me; unfortunately he is an utterly untamed personality." A friend described Beethoven as "singing, howling, stamping, looking as if he had been in mortal combat" while composing; a woman whom the composer courted characterized him as "half-crazy." Beethoven's oddness was accentuated by the loss of hearing that began to afflict him sometime around his 30th birthday in 1800 and rendered him totally deaf by the 1820s. It left him more alone than ever with the torments and delights of his muse, but it did not lessen his creative powers. Although his relentless originality could be a trial to his contemporaries—"they are not for you, but for a later age," Beethoven chided a listener who expressed difficulty in understanding one of his quartets—Beethoven's symphonies, sonatas, and quartets, as well as his glorious piece of sacred music *Missa solemnis* (his favorite of all his works), are without equal. After his death in 1827, a throng followed his coffin to the grave. It was an unprecedented public homage for a composer.

1848

In the years following the demise of Napoléon, republican sentiment in Germany, as elsewhere on the Continent, continued to grow. The German princes, like hereditary monarchs elsewhere, alternately cracked down on liberalism and granted concessions when to do so was either absolutely necessary or essentially painless. In 1848, as had happened some 50 years earlier, a revolution in France ignited changes throughout Europe. In February of that

(continued on page 73)

SCENES OF
GERMANY

66

Overleaf: The Hauptbahnhof, or main train station, of Hamburg is among Germany's busiest and most efficient railway stations. Germany has more than 27,320 miles (43,960 kilometers) of railway lines.

A streetcar drives through Bonn, the birthplace of the composer Ludwig van Beethoven (1770–1827).

In the 1980s, a West German enjoys an international selection of record albums. Today, eastern Germany is also gaining wide access to consumer goods.

At right, Berlin's Kurfürstendamm, the thoroughfare that has become the center of international life in the city, ripples with neon lighting. In the center, the ruin of the neo-Romanesque Kaiser-Wilhelm-Gedächtniskirche, a church built in memory of Kaiser Wilhelm I in 1895, has been kept as a reminder of the destruction of war. The ruin stands between the new church and its campanile.

A man and woman work in a field of pansies near Cologne in the Rhine Valley. Among Cologne's prominent industries are chocolate and perfume—the city has given its name to the well-known toilet water Eau de Cologne that was first made by the Italian chemist Giovanni Farina, who settled in Cologne in 1709.

A steelworker wears protective clothing at the Thyssen steel plant in Duisburg, in the industrial region of the Ruhr. Duisburg, located where the Ruhr and Rhine rivers meet, is the largest inland port in Europe; its abundant raw materials, especially iron, have made Duisburg the center of the steel industry.

Students work in a physics lab at the Technical University of Berlin. After high school students pass their Abitur examination, they are guaranteed admission to a university.

The wildest and steepest bank of the Rhine is the right bank, from Rüdesheim to Koblenz. Each castle, island, and rock along the Rhine has its own tale of chivalry or legend, including (center) the Lorelei rock and (left) Castle Katz (Cat) near St. Goarshausen. Because of the Lorelei's famous echo and its threat to river navigation, it has been immortalized by German poets as a siren who by her song has lured sailors to their death. Castle Katz, whose name derives from its builders, the counts of Katzenelnbogen, is said to have been constructed to counter the Mäuserturm (Mouse Tower) built farther downstream.

The serene courtyard of Castle Church in Wittenberg is a popular tourist spot.

The citizens of Altenburg (near Bamberg) raise barricades to try to force the duke to accept a liberal constitution during the German revolution of 1848. The German Confederation met in Frankfurt to unite Germany under a constitutional republican government but failed to do so when Prussia's king Friedrich Wilhelm IV refused to accept restrictions on his absolute power.

(continued from page 64)

year, French republicans overthrew the so-called citizen king, Louis Philippe, and proclaimed a republic. The revolt was followed by similar uprisings in most of the kingdoms of Europe. In Germany, members of all classes took to the streets; the fighting was particularly fierce in Prussia. The stunned princes were forced to grant concessions, and at the insistence of the aroused German populace the Diet of the Confederation was abolished in favor of a popularly elected national assembly. Plans for the establishment of a united, constitutional monarchy were drawn up, but although

28 of the German states approved of the proposal, the two most powerful, Austria and Prussia, proved problematic. The proposal was doomed to failure without the participation of at least one of those two states, but considerable opposition was voiced against including the many non-German subjects of the Habsburgs in the new German state. Furthermore, the compromise solution of simply denying them voting rights and other civil liberties was unacceptable to the republicans because it violated the very principles they had risen up to establish. It was then hoped that Prussia's king, Friedrich Wilhelm IV, could be prevailed upon to accept the crown of a united, constitutional Germany, but the monarch was affronted by the very notion of constitutional checks upon his absolute power. His right to rule was given by God to the Hohenzollerns, Friedrich Wilhelm IV asserted, and he refused to accept "a diadem molded out of the dirt and dregs of revolution, disloyalty, and treason." After Friedrich Wilhelm IV's refusal, the revolution lost its momentum. Little of lasting significance was achieved; ultimately, the Confederation and the Diet were restored under Austria's control, and those rebels who remained discontented were forced into submission at bayonet point.

Blood and Iron

Tragically, when German unification was at last attained, it was achieved not as the product of the movement to establish constitutional republican government but as a consequence of a renewed commitment to authoritarianism in Prussia. In September 1862, King Wilhelm I found himself at an impasse with his country's parliament over the military budget and reorganization of the armed services. Wilhelm I wanted more of his citizenry to serve compulsory periods in the army, and he increased funds to modernize the military; the parliament, known in Prussia as the *Landtag*, opposed both proposals. Neither side was willing to give in, so Wilhelm I summoned the only man he believed could break the deadlock, a 47-year-old civil servant and diplomat, Otto von Bismarck, and named him prime minister.

Bismarck wasted little time in letting the Landtag know how he felt about democracy and legislators who would dare defy the king. "The great questions of the day will not be settled by speeches and majority votes," he told the Prussian parliament in his first address to them, "but by blood and iron." Bismarck believed completely in the authority of the state as represented by the king and even said once, "I feel I am serving God when I serve the King." When the parliament refused to yield on the military budget issue, Bismarck simply dissolved it and governed without legislative authority. The military was enlarged, as Wilhelm I had wished, and under Bismarck's leadership Prussia embarked on an industrialization program that greatly increased its productive capacity.

Bismarck's greatest concern was the expansion of Prussian power. When Austria called for a conference of all the German

Otto von Bismarck, appointed prime minister of Prussia in 1862, took only eight years to unify Germany by blood and iron. Later called the Iron Chancellor, Bismarck dominated the German Reich until he was asked to resign by Kaiser Wilhelm II in 1890.

Helmuth von Moltke, chief of the Prussian army general staff in the war with Austria, planned the Austrian war with amazing precision. He took full advantage of Prussia's rail system and superior weapons technology and kept his forces mobile and ready to attack at a moment's notice. It took Prussia only seven weeks to defeat Austria.

princes and monarchs, Bismarck interpreted it as an attempt to increase Austrian influence at the expense of Prussia and prevailed upon Wilhelm I, who was flattered by Austria's invitation to attend, not to participate. Thereafter, relations between Austria and Prussia deteriorated, a course of affairs encouraged by Bismarck, who recognized that Prussia could only become the indisputable leading power in Germany by reducing Austrian influence. Friction between the two soon led to outright belligerence as Bismarck sought to provoke a war, a stratagem that proved successful in the summer of 1866. Led by the brilliant general Helmuth von Moltke, the Prussian forces—who held a great advantage in firepower because of their modern armaments and in mobility because of the superb Prussian railway system—crushed the Austrians in seven short weeks. Although Bismarck agreed with the famous Prussian military strategist Karl von Clausewitz that war should be conducted ruthlessly—"Nothing should be left an invaded people but their eyes for weeping," he once proclaimed—he also held, as did Clausewitz, that war should be fought to obtain a specific purpose, as a continuation of diplomacy by other means. Accordingly, the peace with Austria was generous, for Bismarck had already obtained what he wanted. Austria surrendered no territory to Prussia, but the German Confederation was dissolved and Austria's influence in German affairs effectively ended.

Bismarck's way was now clear to unify Germany under Prussian control. Victory over Austria had brought with it popularity and acclaim, and a newly formed parliament contained many Bismarck supporters where previously scarcely a one was to be found. Only four German states—Bavaria, Baden, Württemberg, and Hesse-Darmstadt—now remained outside the Prussian orbit, and Bismarck was certain that they would rally round should he succeed in provoking a war with France, which regarded powerful Prussia as a menace. He got his war in the summer of 1870 by releasing to the press a carefully doctored telegram that made it appear as if Wilhelm I had cavalierly delivered a humiliating insult to the French ambassador. Bismarck's famous "Ems telegram" (Ems was the resort town from which the telegram was sent) obtained the desired result, and France attacked Prussia. Like the Austrian forces, the French army was no match for the steely Prussian infantry and the genius of Moltke, but this time it took several months, not several weeks, before Prussia reigned triumphant.

On January 18, 1871, the German Empire was proclaimed in the Hall of Mirrors at Louis XIV's palace of Versailles. Bismarck had indeed obtained his desire, for the four holdout German states had been swept up into the new German empire and Wilhelm I had accepted the crown as the united Germany's *kaiser* (emperor, derived from Caesar). This time, however, many Germans wondered if the cost had been too high. There was little doubt that the unification of Germany was a monumental event. According to the great British statesman Benjamin Disraeli, the war with France and the accompanying unification constituted a "German revolution, a greater political event than the French Revolution of the last century." Disraeli further lamented that "the balance of power has been entirely destroyed." In the center of Europe, Germany, *das Land der Mitte* (the country in the middle), now boasted the most powerful army in the world. Of the European nations, its population was second only to Russia's, and its industrial productivity trailed only that of Great Britain. But Crown Prince Friedrich, the kaiser's son, wondered if Germany's unification had been purchased at a terrible moral expense. "We are no longer looked upon as the innocent victims of wrong, but rather as arrogant victors," the crown prince confided to his diary. Once Germany had been a "nation of thinkers and philosophers, poets and artists, idealists and enthusiasts," he wrote. Now the world regarded it as "only a nation of conquerors and destroyers, to which no pledged word, no treaty, is sacred, and which speaks with rude insolence of those who have done it injury. . . . We are neither loved nor respected, but only feared."

The Iron Chancellor

Bismarck dominated the German Reich (empire) until his removal by Kaiser Wilhelm II in 1890. Although nominally a parliamentary monarchy with a bicameral legislature whose lower house, the *Reichstag*, was elected by universal suffrage for males over 25 years of age, Germany was one of the most autocratic states in Europe. Bismarck, the chancellor, could be removed only by the emperor, and as long as Wilhelm I lived, he continued to place absolute confidence in the architect of German unification. Those who opposed Bismarck realized full well just how much power he commanded. The leader of the socialists, Wilhelm Liebknecht, criticized the Reichstag's lack of influence, calling it the "fig-leaf of absolutism." The historian Theodor Mommsen was even more outspoken in his denunciations of the "pseudo-constitutional absolutism under which we live and which our spineless people has inwardly accepted."

Bismarck was ruthless in stamping out opposition, particularly the Socialists and the Catholics, who were fearless in their resistance to Prussian domination of Germany, but he showed a surprising tactfulness in his foreign diplomacy, which was based on his awareness of the uneasiness that a strong and united Germany roused in the rest of Europe. Thus, even while Germany began to challenge Britain and France by acquiring colonies overseas, in Africa and the South Pacific, Bismarck succeeded in isolating France diplomatically and preventing it from consummating an alliance against Germany. At home, Bismarck's sense of realpolitik enabled him to make concessions that, had they come from anyone else, would have been hailed as triumphs of liberalism—chiefly, the creation of comprehensive social legislation, including state-sponsored health insurance, pensions, and life and disability insurance that were the first of their kind in the world. But even

The territory of Cameroon in west Africa becomes a German colony in 1884. Under Bismarck's guidance, Germany began to compete with Britain and France in acquiring colonies overseas. Unfortunately, the cost of protecting and administering the colonies far exceeded what little trade Germany had with them.

though the German government exhibited such laudable concern for the welfare of its citizens, it continued to deny the vast majority of them any real measure of self-government.

The Great War (1914–18)

Wilhelm II became kaiser in June 1888, 99 days after the death of his grandfather, Wilhelm I. (Wilhelm I's son, Friedrich III, died after only 99 days in power.) He was determined to rule, not merely to reign, and to achieve that end he soon decided that Bismarck would have to go. The nearly 75-year-old Iron Chancellor remained unyielding to the end, boasting that "there is only one master in this country and I am it" and forcing the kaiser to demand his resignation twice before tendering it.

In the two dozen years that followed Bismarck's fall from grace, Germany continued to thrive. Its population increased by a third, to 68 million, its steel production surpassed Great Britain's, and it became one of the world's foremost economic and financial powers. Bismarck had always dealt from strength, but he had been keenly aware of its limits and had always been exceedingly careful to maintain the friendship of Russia, to keep France diplomatically isolated, and to avoid overtly antagonizing Great Britain even while allying Germany with Italy and Austria-Hungary. Kaiser Wilhelm II was less adept at the subtlety of international affairs. He initiated a policy of rapid naval expansion, carried out at the same time that he was joyfully proclaiming Germany's intention to challenge the British Empire for colonies and worldwide influence. His saber rattling drove Britain, France, and Russia into a defensive alliance, the Triple Entente. (Germany's arrangement with its allies was known as the Triple Alliance.) This division of Europe into two hostile camps was something Bismarck had scrupulously tried to prevent.

When the heir to the Austro-Hungarian throne, Archduke Franz Ferdinand, was assassinated by a Serbian extremist in June 1914,

Austria-Hungary, backed by its ally Germany, pressed a series of humiliating demands on Serbia. Russia, which had styled itself as the protector of the Orthodox peoples of the Balkans, pledged its support for Serbia; France assured Russia that should Germany declare war, the French would stand by the Russians. No one was willing to back down, and war was soon declared. Italy and the Ottoman Empire joined Germany and Austria-Hungary; Britain entered the war on the side of France and Russia when the German forces violated Belgium's neutrality on their way to invading France. It is possible that a cautious approach by the governments of any of the belligerent powers might have enabled war to be averted, but none of the parties involved exercised such prudence. Wilhelm, by this point unafraid of provocative gestures, was unwilling to counsel Austria to exercise restraint, and England, France, and Russia welcomed an opportunity to chasten Germany, whose newfound power made it something of an upstart in the eyes of longer established nations.

Bismarck's diplomatic strategy had been based on the premise that a war on two fronts—its eastern and western borders—would be an unmitigated disaster for Germany, but the more reckless diplomacy of Wilhelm II envisioned a scenario under which Germany could triumph in such a struggle, with which it was now faced. This plan called for a lightning attack on and quick victory over the French in the west, after which matériel, manpower, and resources could be shifted to the east for the war with Russia. As chief of staff, Helmuth von Moltke, nephew and heir of the great hero of Bismarck's wars, and then Erich von Falkenhayn attempted to enact this strategy, but the invasion of Belgium and France left Germany's supply lines dangerously overextended and the offensive soon bogged down. Although both sides suffered appalling casualties—for example, the battles of Verdun and the Somme, in early 1916, cost each side 1 million dead or wounded—after Germany's initial thrust, neither was able to gain territory. For three years, between 1914 and 1917, the western front moved less than 10 miles. In the east, Generals Paul von Hindenburg and Erich von Ludendorff led the German forces to a couple of early victories, but the Russians rallied and held.

Because Germany's strategy was predicated on a quick victory, this stalemate was disastrous, as Germany lacked the resources to fight a prolonged two-front war. Recognizing this, Falkenhayn hoped that Germany's diplomats could negotiate a favorable peace. Hindenburg, as chief of the general staff, and Ludendorff, as quartermaster general, succeeded Falkenhayn in early 1917, and were less realistic, believing that the enormous sacrifice of life Germany had already endured could be justified by nothing less than complete victory. Their attempt to impose a naval blockade on their opponents by means of unrestricted submarine warfare directed against the shipping of even neutral nations brought the United States into the war on the side of the Allies (France and Great Britain). By early 1918, despite recent military successes, Germany was exhausted, and even Generals Hindenburg and Ludendorff recognized that defeat was inevitable. Military collapse led to the downfall of the government, as an uprising of workers, joined in some areas by soldiers and sailors, drove Wilhelm II into exile. The terms of the armistice signed by Germany's new republican government on November 11, 1918, called for its complete disarmament; and by the terms of the Treaty of Versailles, signed on June 28, 1919, in the Hall of Mirrors at Versailles, Germany was held responsible for the Great War and called upon to pay $33 billion in reparations to the victorious Allies. It lost all colonies in Africa and the Far East, Alsace-Lorraine, Posen, parts of Schleswig and Silesia, and its coal mines in the Saar basin. The Covenant of the League of Nations was also written into the treaty. The League was created under the leadership of U.S. president Woodrow Wilson, and it was hoped that this international

German troops in trenches take advantage of a lull in the fighting during World War I. The war lasted 4 years, took the lives of millions of Germans, and left millions more wounded.

organization would guarantee the security of all nations by resolving any further threats to peace.

The human cost of the war had been great. Sixty-five percent of Germany's 11 million fighting men had been killed, wounded, captured, or were missing at war's end. For both sides combined, the casualties totaled more than 37 million.

Expressionism

On August 11, 1919, Germany became a constitutional republic. It had been humiliated by defeat, the terms of the Treaty of Versailles, demilitarization, and loss of its colonies. For many, radical solutions seemed to offer the only hope to rebuild Germany. Some advocated the violent overthrow of capitalism, while others turned to extreme nationalism. Expressionism, a movement in art, architecture, literature, and film, reached its peak in Germany in the years after the war and seemed to mirror the extreme emotions prevalent at the time, which were in themselves a response to the traumatic events Germany had recently undergone.

The term *Expressionism* refers to a manner of writing and painting that utilized the distortion and stylization of forms for the purpose of expressing a highly subjective vision of reality. In the German art world, for example, in 1905 a group of artists in Dresden, calling themselves Die Brücke (The Bridge), had taken up a style of painting characterized by strong, violent contrasts in color and the distortion of shapes and proportions of objects. Such artists as Ernst Ludwig Kirchner, Emil Nolde, and Max Pechstein determined to work toward a better future for humanity by using painting as their medium. They were influenced by late medieval German woodcuts and by primitive art, and they emphasized instinct and spontaneity in their works. In 1911, another group of artists, located in Munich, went beyond the precepts of Die Brücke to free art from the constraints of reality and, eventually, opened the way to abstraction. Calling themselves Der Blaue Reiter (The Blue Horseman), Wassily Kandinsky, Franz Marc, and Paul Klee, among others, professed that freedom of experimentation and originality were essential to their aesthetics. In German literature, especially poetry, Expressionism was heavily influenced by the psychological theories of Sigmund Freud and emphasized subconscious emotion, intuition, and memory. Franz Kafka, Georg Trakl, Franz Werfel, and Ernst Stadler were among the writers who examined the themes of death, decay, and the misery of civilization in their works. In architecture, Walter Gropius and others founded a school of architecture and applied arts, called the Bauhaus, at Weimar in 1919. The Bauhaus was instrumental in establishing a relationship between design and industry in which the design process was based on mass production. Students were trained both as designers and craftspeople, and the idea of the cooperation of all the arts to create an "integrated" work of art was revived, as had once been taught by the late 19th-century Englishman William Morris. (In 1925 the Bauhaus was moved to Dessau; it was dissolved in 1933 by the National Socialist regime.)

After the Great War, the medium of film exemplified the climax of expressionistic thought and imagery in Germany. In the film *The Cabinet of Dr. Caligari* (1919), produced by Rudolf Meinert and directed by Robert Wiene, the use of distorted settings—wedge-shaped doors and oblique windows with crooked frames—and heavy shadows created a state of anxiety and terror that intensified the point of view of the major character, who is insane. Unusual camera angles, moving cameras, fast and slow motion, special lighting effects, and exaggerated close-ups are characteristic of German filmmaking during this period. The use of such techniques made *Caligari* a pivotal work in the history of film, and it greatly influenced such important filmmakers as F. W. Murnau (*Nosferatu*, 1922), Fritz Lang (*Dr. Mabuse the Gambler*, 1922), and Paul Leni (*Waxworks*, 1924).

The Weimar Republic (1919–33)

The legislature of the new German republic met at Weimar, thereby consciously associating itself with the glory days of the German cultural revival, but it was plagued with problems from the outset. The revolution that had overthrown Kaiser Wilhelm II left Germany in a state of virtual anarchy, and when the government of the Weimar Republic proved unable to deal effectively with the country's ruinous economic problems, its doom was virtually assured. When, in the years immediately following the war, Weimar resorted to printing unsecured paper money instead of raising taxes to solve its economic problems, catastrophic inflation resulted. The German mark became worthless, ultimately plunging to 4 trillion to a single dollar. Prices rose hourly, and it was not unusual to see a family transporting its entire life savings to the market in a wheelbarrow in order to buy groceries. Personal fortunes were wiped out overnight; scores of banks, businesses, and corporations failed. Perhaps because there was so little tradition of democratic government in Germany, many were unwilling to give

After World War I, the poor in Berlin lined up to receive a free bowl of soup. Germany struggled under the terms of the Treaty of Versailles: It had to pay more than $33 billion in reparations to the Allies; was demilitarized and occupied by foreigners; and suffered from a severe food shortage.

the Weimar Republic much time to cope with the massive and myriad problems it faced. Its failure to restore economic order seemed proof of its ineffectuality to many Germans, and it was argued that what was needed to solve Germany's crisis was strong leadership. The inability of the Weimar leaders to deal with the crisis left them thoroughly discredited, and the election of the nearly 80-year-old field marshal Hindenburg as president in 1925 signaled the onset of a conservative reaction that would ultimately plunge Germany—and the world—into an unspeakable tragedy.

The Third Reich

Hindenburg had survived the Great War and its aftermath with his reputation as a hero unscathed. Seemingly forgotten were the hundreds of thousands of dead in the mud and trenches at Ypres, the Somme, the Marne, and at Verdun; enshrined in legend were his victories at Tannenberg and the Masurian Lakes. Not surprisingly, as president, Hindenburg encouraged this lack of critical reflection on Germany's recent past by propagating the myth that Germany had not been defeated militarily but had been "stabbed in the back"; that is, betrayed by craven politicians into surrendering. This notion did almost as much as the economic crisis, which worsened with the worldwide depression, to discredit the Weimar Republic, for of course it was republicans, not Wilhelm II, who had signed the armistice.

The resentment that Germans felt about being made the scapegoats for the Great War was played upon masterfully by a politician named Adolf Hitler, an Austrian by birth, a failed artist turned spellbinding orator who in 1919 joined the German Workers party, which he unified, built up, and renamed the National Socialist German Workers, or Nazi, party in 1920. A demonic master of group psychology, Hitler convinced his ever-increasing group of supporters that the blame for Germany's current straits belonged elsewhere—with the politicians who had sold it out at the end of World War I; with the leaders of the Allies, who had self-servingly affixed all the blame for the Great War on Germany; with the Communists, who wished to infect Germany with the noxious dogma of Karl Marx, whose doctrine of worker control of the means of production was despised by most Germans; with the Jews, who controlled Germany's finance and were thus deemed responsible for the economic crisis and who were foreigners and outsiders who "tainted" Germany's racial purity. Making cunning use of German myth and legend, Hitler promised a rebirth of German greatness, the creation of a Third Reich that would last 1,000 years. (The Holy Roman Empire, from 962 to 1806 was considered the First German Reich, Bismarck's Second Reich lasted from 1871 to 1918, and Hitler's Third Reich began in 1933.)

The German people were ready to accept any solution that offered an end to their problems and a restoration of Germany's prestige. Democracy, as judged by the performance of the Weimar government, had failed, and communism was anathema to a large

Adolf Hitler passes cheering crowds in Czechoslovakia and merges the country with the Third Reich in 1939. Hitler mesmerized crowds with his fiery speeches and appeared in awe-inspiring theatrical settings, and he launched an intense propaganda campaign to sway the public to his side.

segment of the population. Although Hindenburg was reelected president in 1932—Hitler finished second—it was apparent that the Nazis claimed a great degree of support from all segments of society. In January 1933, Hindenburg, despite severe personal misgivings, asked Hitler to become chancellor, recognizing that the cooperation of the Nazis was necessary if the government was to function at all and hoping that some way could still be found to control Hitler. Two months later, the eligible German electorate voted in the parliamentary elections, giving the Nazis a more than two-to-one advantage over the next most numerous party in the Reichstag, as the Weimar parliament was known. Several weeks later, the Reichstag passed the Enabling Act, which combined with subsequent legislation essentially dissolved the republic and gave Hitler sweeping dictatorial powers. Among the laws that Hitler then promulgated were a series of measures depriving Jews of virtually every civil liberty and privilege. (For purposes of this legislation, even a person who was married to a Jew or who had one Jewish grandparent was defined as a Jew.) Over time, this policy was expanded to a program that called for the systematic imprisonment and murder of every Jew in Germany and, ultimately, on the European continent.

It is certainly beyond the ability of a short work to begin to explain how a nation could have acquiesced in the implementation of such an infernal program. Nevertheless, some attempts must be made. Certainly, many of Hitler's followers assumed that his murderous anti-Semitism was simply rhetoric, calculated to win him the support of those who wished to blame the Jews for Germany's problems. Equally as obvious is that a large segment of German society was anti-Semitic, and the roots of anti-Semitism ran deep. Stripping Jews of all their property, forbidding them to go school or to travel or trade, and seizing all their religious books had been recommended by various factions throughout history. Although prior to Hitler, Germany had been regarded as relatively tolerant in its acceptance of Jews in comparison with many other nations of Europe, the practice of regarding them as something less than human was of long standing. Following the upheaval of the war and the Weimar years, many Germans were apparently willing to countenance the severest measures, including mass murder, against a segment of German society if, as Hitler promised, those measures would restore the Germany they had known. When, by about 1939, it became apparent that Hitler indeed intended to carry out even his most unspeakable plans, Germans were also able to say, many of them proudly, that Hitler had fulfilled all of his other promises as well—he had reduced unemployment, ended the chaos of the Weimar period, strengthened German industry, renounced the Treaty of Versailles, restored the German military, created a new Reich that included the German-speaking peoples of Austria and Czechoslovakia, and presided over a rebirth of German power and prestige. To their nation's eternal shame, for many Germans this justified the *Führer* (leader; the title assumed by Hitler) in all else that he did. For others, by the time they awoke to the full horror of what had occurred, it was too late—Hitler was too firmly entrenched in power.

At that point, many Germans were simply too frightened to speak out or resist. Still others cultivated ignorance, later claiming that no one really knew about the concentration camps. It should also be noted that there were many brave Germans who did resist Hitler. This resistance took the form of both public opposition and private acts of almost unfathomable courage. Nevertheless, the opposition was always very small, and the sheer magnitude of what Hitler's Germany carried out—war against most of Europe and the United States and the systematic extermination of 6 million Jews, along with Poles, Gypsies, and other

A banner erected in 1936 by the Nazis in Gryfice, Pomerania (now in northwestern Poland), states that Germans do not buy from Jews. Such economic boycotts and other restrictive measures were the prelude to Hitler's program of mass extermination.

groups considered inferior—would not have been possible without widespread acceptance at all levels of society.

Hitler's conception of his Reich included Austria and the Sudetenland (the German-speaking portion of Czechoslovakia), so in 1938 he convinced Austria to reunite with Germany and cajoled the leaders of Britain and France into allowing him to seize the Sudetenland. Still not content, he occupied Czech-speaking lands in early 1939 and turned Slovakia into a puppet state. Then, in September 1939, Hitler invaded Poland, and Britain and France at last declared war on Germany.

France fell quickly to the German *Blitzkrieg*, or lightning war, which employed tanks and dive bombers to spread rapid destruction and to shock and confuse the enemy. Britain struggled on alone, until Hitler's invasion of the Soviet Union in June 1941 brought that nation into the war. The United States entered the war in December 1941 following a sneak attack on Pearl Harbor, Hawaii, by Japan, Germany's ally.

As powerful as it was, Germany did not possess the industrial capacity to support a war of such magnitude. When the tide began to turn against Germany, Hitler became increasingly unresponsive to the facts of the military situation, insisting that loyal Germans must fight to the death. By the spring of 1945, Russian forces were advancing across Germany from the east while American, British, and French troops drove in from the west. Ensconced in his fortified bunker in Berlin, Hitler finally had to admit the collapse of the Third Reich. On April 29, 1945, he married his long-time mistress, Eva Braun, in the bunker. The following day, both of them committed suicide. Germany capitulated a few days later.

Jubilant Berliners wave to a U.S. Air Force transport plane as it airlifts supplies to the city. In 1948, in retaliation against policies of the Western Allies, the Soviet Union blockaded the roads leading to the Western-controlled sectors of Berlin. The Allied airlift, which lasted more than 11 months, carried nearly 1.6 million tons of food, clothing, medicine, and coal to the beleaguered city.

5

From Rubble to Reunion

Germany emerged from World War II with many of its cities demolished, its economy in ruins, and millions of its citizens homeless and starving. Moreover, it was occupied by the four victorious Allied powers—the United States, France, Great Britain, and the Soviet Union. As a result of agreements made at the Yalta and Potsdam conferences during the war, Germany was partitioned into four sectors. The capital city, Berlin, although located deep within the Soviet zone, was also divided among the four occupiers.

A program of denazification, designed to remove from positions of responsibility all persons with past Nazi ties, was introduced in all the German zones, although its effectiveness varied. All four Allies also cooperated in carrying out the war-crimes trials at Nuremberg, at which 12 of Hitler's leading advisers were sentenced to death.

Initially, the Allies had agreed that the Germans should never again possess the ability to carry out aggressive war against the rest of Europe. For a time, the United States, which emerged from the war as the leading world power, contemplated imposing the Morgenthau Plan, named for its creator, Henry Morgenthau, Jr., secretary of the Treasury under President Franklin D. Roosevelt. Morgenthau proposed crippling Germany's industrial capacity by dismantling all its factories, reasoning that a nation without the ability to mass-produce armaments and other industrial goods could never contemplate waging war.

But as it became apparent that Joseph Stalin, the leader of the Soviet Union, intended to transform the countries of Eastern Europe into Soviet satellites, the Allied emphasis shifted from German containment to helping Germany recover its economic health. The best protection against future German aggression, according to this new line of thinking, was to ensure that a prosperous postwar Germany developed along genuinely democratic lines.

Because Stalin had no intention of allowing a united, revitalized Germany to align itself with the West, a break between the Soviet Union and the rest of the Allies was inevitable. The immediate cause was the issue of economic policy. As had been the

Signs of division: In 1949 a bicyclist stops to look at the boundary notice in the British sector of Berlin near the Brandenburg Gate. Berlin had been divided into four sectors, mirroring the division of the country as a whole.

Refugees from eastern Germany fill the ruined streets of Berlin in 1945. Three years later, when the Allies lifted economic controls over the western sectors of Germany, new productivity and employment brought those areas back to life.

case in the early days of the Weimar Republic, Germany's economy was in chaos. Hoarding was rampant and food was scarce; what little was available could be obtained only on the black market. Although much of Germany's productive capacity remained intact, economic incentive was dampened by the stringent wage and price controls remaining from the Nazi era.

Ludwig Erhard, one of a number of remarkable postwar German leaders, became economic director of the British and American occupied zones, with which the French zone soon merged. Erhard overcame American skepticism, insisting that all price controls and rationing be eliminated. The transition from a state-directed to a free-market economy initially resulted in even greater shortages and higher prices, but these rapidly gave way to stability, renewed productivity, and full employment.

In 1948, the first year of the reforms, production in the non-Communist zones rose by 50 percent; then it increased by 25 percent the following year. According to economist Henry Wal-

The division of Germany after World War II. The zones controlled by the United States, Britain, and France coalesced into West Germany; the Soviet-controlled zone evolved into East Germany. West Berlin became a detached Western area deep within East Germany.

lich, the new policies "transformed the German scene from one day to the next. . . . The gray, hungry, dead-looking figures wandering about the streets in their everlasting search for food came to life."

Meanwhile, the Soviets were determined to place their own political stamp on the zone under their control. Like the rest of the Eastern European nations liberated from the Nazis by Soviet troops, the Soviet zone of Germany was to become a Communist society, controlled by the state in all major aspects of life and dominated, both politically and militarily, by the Soviets.

With good cause, the Soviets saw the new economic policies in the Western Allied zones as the first step toward unification of those areas. The Soviets responded in 1948 by cutting off all land routes into the Western-controlled sectors of Berlin. The Western powers responded with an airlift of food and other necessities to the beleaguered Berliners. By the time the Soviets lifted their blockade in the spring of 1949, the Allies and most Germans were convinced of the impossibility of immediately reunifying Germany. Instead, Germany was subjected to a new, longer-lasting division: The Federal Republic of Germany (West Germany) was formed from the American, British, and French zones, with its capital at Bonn. The Soviet zone became the German Democratic Republic (East Germany), with its capital at East Berlin. West Berlin remained an isolated Western outpost.

At the end of the war, much of the easternmost territory claimed by Germany had been returned to Poland or Czechoslovakia. Of what remained, West Germany occupied slightly more than two-thirds—about 96,000 square miles (248,640 square kilometers). East Germany covered about 41,000 square miles (106,190 square kilometers). Forty-seven million people lived in West Germany, 18 million in East Germany. Every fifth member of the West German population was a refugee, either from East Germany or from the former German regions farther to the east.

Developments in West Germany

West Germany's constitution, the Basic Law, was conceived as a transitional arrangement, meant to hold until reunification could be achieved. However, it turned out to be a lasting document that serves the united Germany of today.

The Basic Law established a federal German nation, the *Bundestaat*, governed by a parliamentary system. The legislature consists of two houses: The *Bundestag*, or lower house, is elected by direct popular vote of all individuals 18 years of age and older. Normally, a party must win 5 percent of the national vote to gain representation in the Bundestag. The upper house, the *Bundesrat*, includes three to six representatives from each *Land* (state), depending on its population. These representatives are appointed by the Land's parliament.

The head of the German government is the chancellor, who is the leader of the party or coalition of parties that commands a working majority in the Bundestag. The chancellor's government remains in power only so long as that majority is maintained. The head of state is the president, elected by direct popular vote. The president serves a five-year term and can succeed himself or herself only once. The chancellor holds the real power. The president's position is largely ceremonial, though the president can—and often does—wield considerable moral weight.

Germany's federal judiciary consists of the following courts: a Federal Constitutional Court, which ensures a uniform interpretation of the constitution and protects the fundamental rights of citizens as defined in the Basic Law; a high court of justice; and courts with jurisdiction in administrative, financial, labor, and social matters.

Two parties dominated West German politics and have continued their preeminence since reunification: the Christian Democratic Union (CDU) and the Social Democratic Party (SPD). These two parties have supplied all the German chancellors since

World War II. A third and smaller party, the Free Democratic Party (FDP), has often served as the "swing" party in forming coalitions and breaking parliamentary deadlocks.

The SPD, with its origins in 1875, draws its greatest support from the working class. Its continued attachment to socialist doctrines after World War II hurt its image, because many people believed that this ideology indicated an unwelcome friendship with the Soviet Union. In 1959, the SPD dropped its commitment to full socialism and began to support private enterprise, although it continued to believe that the government should play a role in providing for an equitable distribution of wealth. Even with this change, the SPD did not have the chance to lead the federal government until 1969.

The CDU, which has long drawn the majority of its support from Catholics (who today make up almost half of the German

Konrad Adenauer, the first chancellor of West Germany and leader of the Christian Democratic Union, set in motion the programs of a "socially responsive free-market economy" and codetermination, in which management and labor became partners in industry.

population), was the paramount force in the first two decades of West German politics. CDU leader Konrad Adenauer, the first West German chancellor, was 73 years old when elected in 1949 and had served in the Reichstag during the Weimar years. Despite his age, he would continue in the chancellor's office for 14 years. He and Erhard implemented their concept of a socially responsive free-market economy, which included judicious government intervention when necessary. Integral to this approach was the concept of *Mitbestimmungsrecht*, or codetermination, which held that management and labor should work as partners in industry.

Despite the challenge of feeding, clothing, and housing millions of refugees from the east, national income rose 112 percent under Adenauer, and wages increased 119 percent by 1956. By 1960, unemployment was less than 1 percent, and there were seven jobs available for every person who wanted one. Adenauer's government also provided its citizens with comprehensive social benefits that included health insurance, pensions, unemployment benefits, and free health care. The economic miracle fed on itself. As the average German became more prosperous, he or she was able to purchase items previously considered luxuries, such as cars, televisions, and other electronic equipment. Industry expanded rapidly to meet this demand, with total output increasing sixfold between 1950 and 1964.

In international affairs, Adenauer's most important contribution was his insistence that Germany break with those elements of the past that had led it to disaster. In particular, he sought to end the age-old enmity between Germany and France, and in 1962 the two nations signed a treaty of friendship. Equally significant were his overtures to Israel, the Jewish homeland created in the aftermath of World War II. On behalf of Germany, Adenauer apologized to the world's Jews for the Holocaust and committed his nation to paying Israel significant reparations for Nazi war crimes.

Erhard followed Adenauer as chancellor in 1963 but remained

in office only until 1966, as West Germany suffered its first economic slowdown. A coalition of the CDU and SPD, headed by Kurt Kiesinger, succeeded Erhard's government until 1969.

The Western Allies officially ended their occupation of West Germany in 1955, leaving it an independent state recognized by most countries (including the Soviet Union, though East Germany held out until 1972). The Allies also allowed West Germany to raise and maintain an army of 500,000, which became one of the best-equipped in Western Europe. West Germany joined the Western defense alliance, the North Atlantic Treaty Organization (NATO), and the reunited Germany remains a NATO member.

Developments in East Germany

East Germany, meanwhile, provided a stark contrast to West Germany. Following World War II, the Soviets had confiscated machinery, livestock, and equipment from the German lands under their control. Private ownership of land and industry was abolished. Farmland was taken from large landholders and redistributed to some 500,000 farmworkers, most of whom toiled in large state-run cooperatives. During this process, many East Germans lost their homes and jobs and were reduced to poverty.

Although the Communist system ultimately provided an even fuller assurance of basic necessities than did the West, all political and economic decisions were carefully controlled by central authorities, and freedoms taken for granted in West Germany were unavailable in the East. Politically, the country remained under the thumb of the Soviet Union, which structured the government along its own lines.

Control of the government and all other positions of power lay firmly in the hands of the Socialist Union party (SED), the German version of the Communist party. Effectively, the party structure merged with that of the government. The first secretary of the SED—a position occupied by Walter Ulbricht from 1953 to 1971—held the most powerful post in the government. Opposing political parties were banned or suppressed, and ballots were not cast in secret. Artistic expression and the media were placed under strict government control.

The Soviets also imposed their system of five-year economic plans, which placed increasing pressure on workers and managers of state-run plants to raise output. In 1953, public anger over job pressure, food shortages, and overall sovietization led to strikes and rioting. Soon after, the Soviets began to cede more power to Germans.

Even with the relaxation of direct Soviet control, however, the drain of population from East to West continued, especially among young men. Combined with war losses, this created a situation in which women far outnumbered men in East Germany. Between 1949 and 1960, 3.5 million citizens fled East Germany, a fact that prompted the government to construct the Berlin Wall in 1961. During the existence of East Germany, over 900 people died attempting to cross the country's borders, which were outfitted with machine-gun towers and patrolled by up to 73,000 East German troops.

Following the completion of the Berlin Wall, East Germany introduced its New Economic System, allowing lower-level workers to make decisions affecting productivity. These changes, along with the retention of the young, educated population that had made up the majority of the escapees before the wall's construction, led to a rapid and dramatic increase in industrial output and standard of living. This economic upswing, however, slowed in the late 1960s.

Steps Toward Cooperation: The 1970s and 1980s

The 1970s brought the two nations closer to accommodation. Willy Brandt, former mayor of West Berlin, became the first SPD chancellor of West Germany in 1969. His main thrust in international relations was his *Ostpolitik* (eastern policy), a reaching out to East Germany and the other nations of Eastern Europe. Reunification, Brandt indicated, was no longer a goal of West German policy.

In 1971, Erich Honecker replaced long-time East German first secretary Walter Ulbricht, after Ulbricht's failure to deal effectively with the economic slowdown. Honecker improved East German working and living conditions—housing became more readily available and consumer goods more affordable. Like Brandt, Honecker appeared determined to ease tensions between the two nations. Soon, they signed agreements to recognize their respective countries, to respect each other's borders, and to ease travel between East and West (and, in particular, to allow unhindered civilian access to Berlin). In 1973, both nations joined the United Nations.

A year later, tensions flared again when it was discovered that one of Brandt's closest advisers was a spy planted by East Germany's ruthlessly efficient intelligence service, the *Stasi*. Brandt, winner of the 1971 Nobel Peace Prize, resigned, to be succeeded by the SPD's Helmut Schmidt, who remained chancellor until 1982. During Schmidt's watch, the West German economy took an uncharacteristic, though mild, downturn, leading to a minor recession in the early 1980s.

The 1970s also witnessed the development of two peculiarly West German activist groups: the Greens, a grassroots group protesting damage to the environment caused by rapid industrialization; and the Baader-Meinhof Gang, an urban terrorist group that attracted world attention by its bombings and bank robberies. Baader and Meinhof both committed suicide before the decade's end. The Greens, however, went on to form a respected environmental political party that still exerts an influence far beyond what its vote-getting ability might suggest.

About the time of Schmidt's ascension, Honecker began to move East Germany toward the Soviets again, erasing some of the gains of the earlier accords. By that time, the East German domestic economy seemed secure: Wages had risen while the cost of living remained artificially low because of state-dictated pricing of housing and food. East Germany boasted the highest standard of living in Eastern Europe and the world's tenth most productive industrial output.

The slippage in the West German economy helped bring the CDU back to power in 1982, under Chancellor Helmut Kohl. Meanwhile, Honecker's renewed tilt toward the Soviets prompted the United States to move nuclear missiles to West Germany in 1983. More important than these developments, however, were the behind-the-scenes changes in the Soviet Union that ultimately destroyed the Soviet system of control.

Throughout the Soviet Union, long years of bureaucratic domination by Moscow had stifled initiative, diverted ever more of the economy to military buildup, and lowered citizen morale. Soviet leadership, ossified under the long rule of Leonid Brezhnev and his short-term successors, temporarily took on new life under the forward-looking Mikhail Gorbachev, who assumed the helm in 1985. He quickly pushed for rapprochement with the West and the lessening of Soviet control in Eastern Europe. However, for the Soviet Union, this proved to be too little, too late. Overburdened and underproductive, the Soviet economy and political structure spiraled out of control. After a brief 1991 attempt at a coup by Moscow hard-liners, the power of Gorbachev and the entire Soviet apparatus lay broken. On December 25, 1991, the Soviet Union—the largest nation ever to exist on earth—dissolved, leaving Russia, its original core, as an economically, militarily, and spiritually shattered successor.

During the latter half of the 1980s, the Communist Eastern European governments became rudderless with the loss of Soviet guidance. They quickly fell prey to citizen dissension and, finally, revolt. In 1989, East Germany imploded. Erich Honecker, terminally ill, was removed as first secretary of the SED in October and replaced by Egon Krenz, who reluctantly relaxed travel restrictions in the hope of stemming the mass exodus of East Germans through Hungary and Czechoslovakia to the West. Instead, the exodus turned into a stampede.

Together Again

When the Berlin Wall fell in November 1989, West Germany was inundated by East Germans fleeing the turmoil of their country. The following March, in its first-ever democratic elections, East Germany voted in a new government that favored reunification. The West was quick to agree. On October 3, 1990, East Germany ceased to exist and was absorbed by West Germany. The reunited Germany, by treaty, renounced nuclear, biological, and chemical weapons and agreed to reduce its armed forces to 370,000. Lastly, it was decided that the government would move from Bonn to Berlin by the turn of the century.

The resulting unified Germany adopted the West German name of the Federal Republic of Germany, along with the West German constitution (the Basic Law), the parliamentary form of government, and the free-enterprise economic system. Helmut Kohl, West German chancellor since 1982, remained head of government. From the West German point of view, the only change in governmental structure was an increase in the number of Länder (states) from 10 to 16. Five states were added from East Germany, and Berlin became a state in itself. Thus, with remarkable smoothness and speed, the Germans put back together the nation that had been chopped apart after World War II.

The Old Music Hall is dwarfed by a modern high rise in Hamburg. Though much of the city was destroyed during World War II, Hamburg today is Germany's media capital and second largest city.

6

The Land, the People, and the Future

Today's Federal Republic of Germany is home to some 84 million people living in an area of 137,826 square miles (356,970 square kilometers), bordered on the west by France, Luxembourg, Belgium, and the Netherlands, on the north by the North Sea, Denmark, and the Baltic Sea, on the east by Poland and the Czech Republic, and on the south by Austria and Switzerland.

Germany comprises three distinct topographical regions: the southern highlands, which include the Alps, Europe's greatest mountain chain; the central uplands, a region of plateaus, hills, forests, and river valleys; and the northern lowland, whose sandy plains, extending to the Baltic Sea, were formed by glaciers thousands of years ago.

The most important interior waterway (central to German folklore) is the Rhine River, with its beautiful valley dotted by ancient castles. Navigable for almost its entire 700-mile (1,129-kilometer) length, it is central to Germany's economy, reaching into the most important industrial and coal-mining region in Europe. Another important river, the Moselle, flows north from France to the German city of Trier and joins the Rhine near Koblenz. Moselle vineyards, south of Koblenz, produce the celebrated Riesling grape used to make a light, dry white wine. The Elbe and Oder river systems flow across the northern plains but do not cut deeply; in fact, the region has no hills higher than 330 feet (100 meters). The Elbe flows northwest into the North Sea. The Oder begins in the Czech mountains and flows north into the Baltic Sea.

The German climate is generally temperate. The west experiences mild winters and summers because of the moist, warm winds that blow in from the Atlantic Ocean. In the central uplands, temperatures are lower than the national average, and rainfall is higher. The average temperature in the northwest is about 50 degrees F (10 degrees C); in the southwest, 53 degrees F (12 degrees C). The east has colder winters and short, hot summers.

In heavily industrial, densely populated western Germany, pollution from industrial waste, fuel emissions, and acid rain is a

Nets are set for catching eels along the North Sea coast in Schleswig-Holstein. The northernmost state in Germany, Schleswig-Holstein shares a border with Denmark.

major problem with political repercussions, as seen by the founding of the Green party. Despite the role of the forest as a setting for much of German literature and folklore, little of the original woodland remains. In the east, which is largely agricultural, most of the natural vegetation has been cleared for crops. Throughout the country, stands of birch and Scotch pine have replaced the oak forests, although in the uplands, including the Thuringian Forest, and in the Alps, the Black Forest, and the Swabian Jura, some original forests of beech, silver fir, and spruce still thrive.

Deer, red squirrel, wild boar, and fox can still be found in the woods. Hare and small rodents, such as the dormouse and hamster, are abundant. Beaver are plentiful in the Elbe valley. Some wild boar live deep in the forests, and occasional bears, wolves, foxes, otters, badgers, and wildcats inhabit remote areas. Such

Like many of the other small cities in Germany, Wittenberg, located on the Elbe River northwest of Berlin, serves as a regional economic and cultural center.

birds as the gray shrike, thrush, nightingale, and nutcracker abound in the north and southeast. The sea eagle and the white stork live along the eastern rivers.

Germany provides most of its own food needs. The main agricultural products are wheat, oats, barley, rye, potatoes, and beets. Fruit trees line many of the roadways in the south.

Though heavily industrialized, Germany is not a nation of huge cities, and in part because of the partition and isolation of Berlin for four decades, it has not developed a truly dominant national center like London or Paris. The combined population of the four largest German cities—Berlin, Hamburg, Munich, and Cologne—is less than that of London or New York. Various cities serve as regional hubs and leaders in different aspects of the urban economy.

A Land of Diversity

Contrary to stereotype, Germany includes considerable diversity. This should not be surprising, considering its long history of fragmentation. Southern Germany is the land seen most often on postcards—a picturesque region of castles, forested hillsides, old churches, and vineyards. The charms of the north, with its cold winters and windswept flatlands, are less obvious. The south is very much a part of the interior of the continent, and the traditional German connection with Austria is apparent there. In the north, the focus is the sea.

The north is predominantly Protestant, the south Catholic. The north tends to be more liberal politically. There is nothing like the ethnic diversity of the United States, but, stereotypically, the Germans of the south are seen as more emotional, outgoing, convivial, and good natured, whereas the northerners are considered more stolid and reserved, businesslike, and frugal. The northerners are more likely to be tall and blond, southerners to be shorter and darker.

Various dialects of German differ considerably. High German (*Hochdeutsch*), the literary language and language of public discourse, is taught in school. Local dialects vary to the extent that a German from Swabia, for example, might have difficulty understanding a conversation in the dialect of Berlin. The Low German (*Plattedeutsch*) of the north is closely related to Dutch.

Berlin

The most visible symbol of unification was the reopening of the Brandenburg Gate between the East and West sides of Berlin. Home to 3.5 million people, Germany's largest city suffered a fractured identity during the 41 years of its division. West Berlin, situated 100 miles (160 kilometers) inside the "enemy" territory of East Germany, rebuilt rapidly following the destruction of World War II and became a major manufacturing center. However, it remained under nominal control of the Allied occupation powers—it sent delegates to the West German legislature, but they could not vote. The eastern sector lagged in reconstruction and shared East Germany's generally somber atmosphere.

Berlin has long been one of the world's great cultural centers. During the Weimar Republic following World War I, for example, Berlin was perhaps the leading theater center in the world, and its nightlife, both exuberant and decadent, knew few equals. Major international avant-garde movements in architecture, sculpture, painting, and crafts used Berlin as their main showcase. Such master scientists as Albert Einstein and Max Planck worked here.

Since the 15th century, Berlin has served as a capital, first of Brandenburg, then of Prussia, then of Germany. During the division between East and West, its eastern sector formed the capital of East Germany. Today, a rebuilt Berlin serves as the designated capital of a united Germany, though the functions of government may not be fully transferred from Bonn until after the turn of the century.

Munich: "Village of a Million"

Germans refer to Munich, the prosperous, traditional capital city of Bavaria, as the Village of a Million. Home to the electronics firm of Siemens, the aerospace contractor MBB, and the auto manufacturer BMW, Munich is an economic hub that, unusual for a German city, draws workers from all around the nation. Most of its residents are not native-born, and according to opinion polls, most Germans would prefer to live in Munich if they had to leave their own cities.

Munich has been home to Germany's best classical opera company, as well as to some of its finest collections of art, such as the Alte Pinakothek, the Bayerisches Nationalmuseum, and the Städtische Galerie. Although tourists at Munich's annual Oktoberfest, an exercise in Teutonic revelry, are likely to encounter beer-quaffing natives attired in the traditional lederhosen (short leather pants) or dirndl (a colorful dress with a tight bodice and full-cut skirt), Munich also offers a sophisticated café nightlife. The nation's finest sports facilities are in Munich, a legacy of 1972 when the city hosted the Olympic Games. Though heavily damaged by Allied bombing during World War II, Munich boasts some of the finest examples of Baroque architecture in Germany.

Stuttgart

Stuttgart is the most important city of Swabia, a region in the southwest in the Land of Baden-Württemberg. Germans as a whole are often stereotyped as slavish adherents to the work ethic. Within Germany, though, it is Swabians who are known for their devotion to hard work, frugality, the Protestant faith, and family. "Work, work, and build your little house" is the traditional Swabian motto.

Frankfurt is Germany's financial center. Goethe, who was born here, called Frankfurt the "secret capital" because of its prosperous and cosmopolitan nature.

Home to Daimler-Benz (the manufacturer of Mercedes Benz autos), Porsche, and the German headquarters of IBM, Stuttgart has been a leading creator and beneficiary of the economic miracle. Yet its citizens, unlike those of Munich, consider it in poor taste to demonstrate their wealth. The city retains something of a pastoral quality. From this region comes much of Germany's wine, and many city dwellers maintain small plots to grow grapes and other fruits and vegetables.

Much of the inner city has been declared a pedestrian zone—an ironic touch in the city where, in 1883, Gottlieb Daimler invented the first vehicle propelled by an internal combustion engine.

"Mainhattan"

Mainhattan is the name critics have given to Frankfurt, a city of about 660,000 people located on the Main River. The slur, as it is considered, is directed primarily at Europe's densest collection of skyscrapers—like those of Manhattan in the United States—but it also pertains to Frankfurt's preoccupation with what Germans consider an American obsession: making money.

Frankfurt is Germany's banking and financial center. It became a financial power in the late 19th century, when it was home to many prominent financiers, including the Rothschilds. Today it is the location of the German stock exchange and most of the country's leading banks. However, its detractors overlook its other myriad attractions, including the Goethe Haus, birthplace and home of the poet and playwright, and a magnificent cathedral, where from 1562 to 1806 the Hapsburg Holy Roman Emperors were crowned. Two of Germany's most influential daily newspapers are published in the city, and the annual Frankfurt Book Fair attracts publishers from around the world.

Hamburg

"A Free and Hanseatic City" is the designation still proudly used by the northern city of Hamburg, Germany's busiest port, second largest city, and media capital. Most television news programs originate in Hamburg, as do the leading weekly news magazines. Like other cities of the German north, Hamburg has suffered somewhat from the recent movement of industry to the south, but its economic base remains sound.

A socialist stronghold since the late 19th century, it was one of the least pro-Nazi cities during the Hitler years. Because it was virtually destroyed twice in one century—by fire in the mid-19th century and by Allied bombs during World War II—Hamburg features some of Germany's most modern architecture. In rebuilding their city, Hamburg residents managed to avoid much of the congestion that characterizes other German urban areas.

As befits its location on the Elbe River near the North Sea, it is a city of bridges—almost 2,200, compared with 400 in Venice, the Italian city famed for its marine setting. The birthplace of composers Felix Mendelssohn and Johannes Brahms, Hamburg maintains a proud cultural tradition, chiefly through its opera house, regarded as Germany's best.

Leipzig

Located in the east central region of Saxony, Leipzig, an 800-year-old city, developed into an international cultural, trading, and industrial center during its East German years. It produces furs, mining ores, chemicals, farm machinery, and printing presses.

The University of Leipzig dates to the early 15th century. The city is also home to many book and sheet-music publishers and to the Deutsches Bucherei, a library that has collected German-language literature for more than 60 years. Like Frankfurt, though on a smaller scale, Leipzig hosts a yearly international book fair.

On Market Square, the 16th-century Altes Rathaus (Old Town Hall) reflects the city's first period of commercial prosperity. Near the square stands St. Thomas Church, where Baroque composer Johann Sebastian Bach lived and worked. Leipzig's musical traditions have been carried on by the St. Thomas Boys' Choir, the Gewandhaus Orchestra, and the College of Music.

Dresden

Like many German cities, Dresden, in the east central part of the country, has been a cultural center for centuries. The Kreuzchor, or Church of the Cross Choir, dates to the Middle Ages. The 19th-century composer Richard Wagner wrote several of his operas while living in Dresden, and nine of Richard Strauss's operas opened there during the early part of the 20th century. The city hosts two symphony orchestras, four theater companies, and many fine art galleries.

A scene in Dresden with the Court Church in the background. This city on the upper Elbe River near the Czech border was devastated by Allied bombing during World War II, but many of its historic buildings have been restored.

An industrial city, Dresden served as the major center for vehicle manufacturing microelectronics, light industry, and food processing under East German rule. Dresden's German Hygiene Museum and the nuclear research center at nearby Rossendorf are important scientific institutions.

Dresden was leveled and thousands killed in 1945 by Allied saturation bombing designed to inspire fear throughout Germany and hasten the war's end—a military approach still debated on moral grounds. However, many of the beautiful historic buildings have been carefully reconstructed. The Zwinger, an 18th-century festival square enclosed by art galleries and other buildings, is the most celebrated example of German Baroque architecture. The Opera House was built between 1871 and 1878 in the Italian Renaissance style, reflecting ancient Greek and Roman architecture.

Education and Economy

In the postwar era, the West German educational system proved adept at preparing its charges to fill the needs of the nation's economy. The same basic system is now taking hold in the former East German territory as well.

At age 10, after four years of primary school, German students are funneled toward either vocational or academic training. The former teaches the student an employable skill or trade, and at age 15 the student begins a part-time apprenticeship. In contrast, those who receive academic training generally stay in school (called *Gymnasium*) until they are 18, then take an examination which, if they pass, virtually guarantees admission to a university. From this academic class Germany draws its professional and intellectual leaders.

The educational process has its drawbacks, most notably the perpetuation of a fairly rigid class system, but the powerful position of German labor unions, the high wages paid to workers, and the German belief in cooperative (as opposed to strictly individual) initiative have helped alleviate the strains that might be expected. A skilled, highly trained, motivated work force has been the most significant German resource.

Overall, the modern German economy has shown a remarkable ability to adapt to changing circumstances. For example, in the 1970s, the Ruhr area, Europe's most important coal-mining and steel-production region, entered a period of decline not unlike that suffered by the so-called Rust Belt of the United States. Recognizing that changing energy and economic needs threatened to make their traditional economic base obsolete, Ruhr leaders began a transition to new industries—petrochemicals, automobile construction, and factories for the production of consumer goods. This flexibility not only averted a major recession, but also proved a buffer during the economic upheaval of unification.

The overall wealth of the country has created a way of life in many respects similar to that of Americans. Germans dress as Americans do and, like Americans, can choose from an incredible variety of consumer items. The country has one of the most sophisticated highway systems in the world, and most German cities, especially in the west, feature excellent public transportation. Consumer electronics are all the rage, just as in the United States. Television, in fact, was credited with a significant role in hastening unification: East Germans could tune in to news shows and other television programs from West Germany, and this increased their awareness of the disparity in the ways of life of the two Germanys.

Today and Tomorrow

Despite the fact that "one Germany" had been a back-burner rallying cry in the West during much of the four decades of separation, reunification was a mixed blessing for both sides. Easterners could expect their overall standard of living to rise over the long run, but in the meantime they forfeited the state-run economy that had provided basic services and assured jobs for its citizens. They also faced the strain of adopting a new political and economic system overnight. The West could claim an ideological victory but was forced to undertake the enormous task of absorbing the weaker Eastern economy, with its lower wages, older industrial base, and crumbling infrastructure—an effort that would dilute the standard of living in the West.

The immediate effect, actually, was a short economic boom, fueled by an increased demand in the East for consumer goods unavailable under Communist rule. Yet, perhaps inevitably, in 1992 Germany experienced an economic setback. Unification strained German public finance, hurt the labor market, and brought to the fore certain existing weaknesses in the economy. The Soviets had supplied East Germany with steel and natural gas, as well as 80 percent of its oil. With these sources gone, eastern industrial output after unification fell to 40 percent of the 1989 level.

Unemployment rose drastically—reaching 18 percent in the east and averaging 10 percent nationally—as workers in the east, formerly assured state-supplied jobs, were forced to compete in an open economy. The German government, dedicated to easing their burden and creating wage parity throughout the country, distributed vast sums of money in maintenance grants. Physical conditions in the east created an enormous drain on the overall economy. Many eastern factories fell far below the environmental standards adopted by West Germany and were inefficient as well. It became clear that these facilities would have to be overhauled or rebuilt.

By the mid-1990s, the economy had recovered, and the hint of a new economic miracle lay in the eastern sector, whose 10 percent growth rate led all of Europe. Total German exports—long the strongest facet of the German economy—rose to $500 billion and continued to outpace imports. In the former East German states, productivity rose from less than half that of the western sector to 68 percent and continued to expand. The total German gross domestic product (the value of all goods and services produced) rose to $2.5 trillion. Economic growth hovered between 1.5 and 2 percent annually, a modest figure, but the inflation rate also remained under 2 percent. As an economic powerhouse in Europe, Germany became one of the leaders in the drive to establish a single European currency.

Certain economic problems remain. The overall unemployment rate in the late 1990s reached its highest level since 1933, and the former East German states will probably require subsidies well into the 21st century. Some German industries have relocated to foreign countries because of high local production costs, stringent government regulation, and high taxes. Still, the

A street in Stralsund offers an example of the reconstruction undertaken in eastern Germany after reunification. Above, the street as it looked in 1990; below, the same block in 1995.

economy remains fundamentally strong and internationally competitive.

Old Animosities Die Hard

Social integration has not come easily since unification. Soon after the East and West rejoined, rising unemployment led to right-wing backlash throughout the country. Much of this anger was turned against foreign "guest" workers, who were seen as taking jobs from Germans. Turks, the largest group of imported workers, became the special victims of hatred and violence.

In a similar response, traditional anti-Jewish sentiment, held in check since World War II, surfaced again. Hate crimes committed against synagogues and Jewish cemeteries increased dramatically; the painting of the banned Nazi swastika and the destruction of gravestones reawakened memories of Hitler's Holocaust. The Basic Law, in one of its few infringements on free speech, bans Nazi propaganda as well as groups or political parties found to be "fundamentally undemocratic," and this restriction has been applied by the courts to both neo-Nazi and Communist parties. Yet the legal deterrents did not eliminate ethnic and religious antagonism.

The mood of resentment peaked in 1992, when the firebombing of a hotel for Turkish immigrants resulted in several deaths. The majority of Germans were appalled by such excesses. A series of candlelight marches culminated in some 500,000 protesters filling Berlin streets to denounce hatred.

In terms of government action, many believe that contemporary Germany has shown strong support of human rights. Since 1949, the German government has sent over 100 billion marks (about $60 billion) to Holocaust victims in the West. Since unification, the Germans have indicated their willingness to pay reparations to Holocaust survivors from Eastern European countries

"Guest" workers from Italy package chocolates in a factory in Cologne. During years of high German unemployment in the early 1990s, such foreign workers, especially Turks, became frequent targets of anger and harassment.

who could not be identified while those countries were under Soviet domination.

On the other side of the ledger, the German government has been taken to task by some observers for its treason trials of former East German officials, who can reasonably claim that they were serving their own country, not attempting to undermine a united Germany that did not then exist. A succession of trials of Kurt Wolff, former head of the notorious East German secret police, the Stasi, seemed motivated largely by frustration over his relentless efficiency in placing spies high in the West German government.

Overall, it appears that the German people have decided to hold the line against those tendencies that once made their country the pariah of 20th-century Europe. Despite the concerns of Germany's former enemies, there is good indication that the new Germany can continue to evolve as a progressive, peaceful, democratic nation.

GLOSSARY

Bundesrat   The upper house of the German legislature.

Bundestag   The lower house of the German legislature, consisting of the delegations from the Länder.

Carolingian Empire   The kingdom presided over by Charlemagne and his ancestors and descendants; at its greatest extent, it included present-day France and Germany.

cold war   The ideological, economic, and political struggle that pitted the United States and its allies against the Soviet Union and its allies for 45 years following World War II.

Führer   German word meaning "leader"; the title assumed by Adolf Hitler.

Hochdeutsch   High German, the national language of public discourse in Germany.

Holocaust   The deliberate extermination by Hitler's government of 6 million European Jews, as well as Gypsies and the mentally and physically deformed.

Holy Roman Empire   The unwieldy, loosely defined political entity conceived as a successor state to the Roman Empire. It lasted from 962 to 1806. Its emperor was considered to be the temporal head of the Roman Catholic church as well as king of the Germans. In reality, the Holy Roman emperors often clashed with the popes and never did unite the many distinct German states.

kaiser   German word meaning "Caesar"; analogous to the Russian word czar, it was the title assumed by Germany's emperors from 1871 to 1918.

Länder   The German word for the 16 individual states that constitute the Federal Republic of Germany.

Mitbestimmungsrecht   Codetermination; that is, the cooperation of ownership, management, and labor in making decisions about the future course of economic institutions and the German economy as a whole.

Nazis   Members of the National Socialist German Workers party led by Adolf Hitler.

Ostpolitik   Literally, "eastern policy"; the term referring to West German chancellor Willy Brandt's policy of reconciliation with East Germany.

realpolitik   A German term adopted into English, referring to politics based on practical rather than ethical or theoretical considerations; a practitioner of realpolitik, such as Bismarck, is likely to give more weight to national interests and power than to conventional conceptions of morality or justice.

Reich   German word meaning "empire." There have been three reichs in German history: The Holy Roman Empire from 962 to 1806; the German empire created by Bismarck in 1871, which lasted until 1918; and Adolf Hitler's self-proclaimed Third Reich, which lasted from 1933 to 1945.

Reichstag   The lower house of the German parliament between 1871 and 1918.

Stasi   The East German secret police, perhaps the most efficient espionage agency of all time.

INDEX

PICTURE CREDITS

Alinari/Art Resource: p. 51; G. Anderson/The Stock Market: p. 67; AP/Wide World Photos: p. 14; The Bettmann Archive: pp. 24, 33, 62, 73, 75, 79, 86, 90; courtesy of German Information Center: pp. 19, 29, 38, 46, 48, 56, 59, 65, 66 (top and bottom), 69 (top and bottom), 76, 95, 99, 106, 108, 109, 113, 116, 120, 122; Giraudon/Art Resource: p. 42; Ellen S. Knudsen: p. 72; Library of Congress: p. 83; Harvey Lloyd/The Stock Market: p. 68; Marburg/Art Resource: p. 44; H. P. Merten/The Stock Market: pp. 70–71; Reuters/Bettmann Archive: p. 18; UPI/Bettmann Archive: pp. 88, 92, 94